100
Best Casseroles
& Stews

100
Best Casseroles
& Stews

The ultimate guide to great casseroles and stews

including 100 delicious recipes

This edition published in 2012
LOVE FOOD is an imprint of Parragon Books Ltd

Parragon
Chartist House
15-17 Trim Street
Bath BA1 1HA, UK

www.parragon.com

ISBN: 978-1-4454-6194-6

Printed in China

Notes for the Reader
This book uses standard kitchen measuring spoons and cups. All spoon
and cup measurements are level unless otherwise indicated. Unless
otherwise stated, milk is assumed to be whole, eggs are large, individual
vegetables are medium, and pepper is freshly ground black pepper.
Unless otherwise stated, all root vegetables should be washed and
peeled prior to use.

The times given are only an approximate guide. Preparation times differ
according to the techniques used by different people and the cooking
times may also vary from those given. Optional ingredients, variations, or
serving suggestions have not been included in the calculations.

Recipes using raw or very lightly cooked eggs should be avoided by
infants, the elderly, pregnant women, and anyone with a chronic illness.
Pregnant and breast-feeding women are advised to avoid eating peanuts
and peanut products. People with nut allergies should be aware that
some of the prepared ingredients used in the recipes in this book may
contain nuts. Always check the packaging before use.

CONTENTS

INTRODUCTION

There is nothing more comforting than a homecooked casserole or stew, whether tender beef and mushrooms immersed in a rich red wine sauce or a filling mixture of spicy vegetables and dried beans.

While we tend to think of casseroles and stews as cold-weather food, there are also many lighter dishes that are ideal for warmer times of year.

What could be more delicious on a summer evening than an aromatic fish and seafood stew eaten alfresco or a colorful medley of Mediterranean vegetables served with fresh crusty bread?

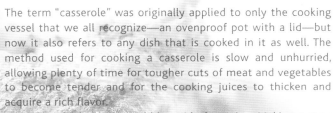

The term "casserole" was originally applied to only the cooking vessel that we all recognize—an ovenproof pot with a lid—but now it also refers to any dish that is cooked in it as well. The method used for cooking a casserole is slow and unhurried, allowing plenty of time for tougher cuts of meat and vegetables to become tender and for the cooking juices to thicken and acquire a rich flavor.

However, the same could be said of stewing. Making a stew might involve using a little more liquid, although not invariably, and is traditionally cooked on the stove instead of in the oven. Stews are generally served in their gravy.

There are many international versions of the casserole and stew, with variations in techniques as well as ingredients. A French daube is a slowly braised dish that was once cooked in a tall casserole dish with a special lid that could be filled with hot charcoal. When suspended over the fire, it benefited from heat from below and above. A Moroccan tagine is a shallow, round earthenware dish with a conical lid that traps steam, thereby making sure that the ingredients are kept moist throughout the long cooking time over a small, round charcoal brazier. Like casserole, the word "tagine" is now applied to the recipe as well as the vessel. Both the daube and tagine can be cooked just as successfully in a casserole dish or Dutch oven in a modern oven. The braised beef dish on page 20 uses traditional stewing techniques, with an Asian twist to the ingredients.

Nowadays, the terms casserole or stew can be applied to a multitude of different dishes, but they are usually one-dish meals with a mixture of ingredients—meat, poultry, fish, vegetables, and even rice or pasta—that are often served in the vessel or gravy in which they are cooked.

They could be cooked in a traditional casserole dish or Dutch oven or a saucepan, stockpot, or baking dish, either on the stove or in the oven. They might be called a casserole, stew, cobbler, hotpot, cassoulet, carbonade, bake, or mole ... the list goes on. Whatever they contain and however they are cooked, there is no denying that casseroles and stews are truly delicious dishes!

hints & tips for success

- A flameproof casserole dish, Dutch oven, or other ovenproof dish can be used to brown meat or other ingredients over a direct heat on the stove before being transferred to the oven to finish cooking. Make sure to choose one with a tight-fitting lid to prevent moisture from being lost during cooking.

- When cutting up meat for a casserole or stew, try to make the pieces the same size to ensure even cooking. If some are much smaller than others, they may overcook and become stringy. Always remove and discard any gristle and trim off excess fat. Unless you're being particularly health conscious, you do not need to remove all marbled fat, because it will add richness and flavor to the cooking juices. If you are worried about fat, the easiest way to make sure that almost all of it is removed is to prepare the casserole or stew the day before it is required, chill it in the refrigerator, and then lift off any fat solidified on the surface before reheating.

- Meat is almost always browned first in order to seal in the juices and give it an attractive brown color. It may be coated in flour, which helps to thicken the cooking juices. Add the pieces of meat to the hot cooking vessel in small batches. Turn them over as soon as they are browned on one side and remove with a slotted spoon when they are sealed all over.

- An easy way to coat pieces of meat with flour is to put them into a plastic food bag, add the seasoned flour, hold the bag closed, and shake well. Shake off any excess flour from the meat before cooking.

- If the sediment in the bottom of the cooking vessel looks as if it might scorch, stir in a little of the recipe's liquid—water, wine, stock, beer, or cider—between sealing batches of meat. Taste and if it isn't burned, set aside to add with the main quantity of liquid later.

- Onions and sometimes other vegetables need to be softened before they are combined with the other ingredients. This is usually best done separately from browning the meat.

- Cooking times in the recipes are always guidelines instead of hard-and-fast rules and you cannot speed up the cooking without catastrophic results. Try to build a little extra time into your schedule so that if your particular batch of meat or dried beans is not tender enough at the recommended time, the family won't faint from hunger when the casserole requires an additional 15–30 minutes in the oven. Do not increase the oven temperature in the vain hope that cooking will speed up.

- Check the quantity of liquid in the stew from time to time during cooking. If it seems to be drying out, stir in a little hot stock or water. If the juices still seem to be a little too runny toward the end of the cooking time, remove the lid to let the excess liquid evaporate and the juices thicken.

- For a fresh bouquet garni, tie 1 fresh thyme sprig, 2 fresh flat-leaf parsley sprigs, and 1 fresh bay leaf together with kitchen string. Use a long piece of string and tie to the handle of the casserole, saucepan, or stockpot so that the bouquet garni dangles into the hot liquid but is easy to remove. Do not forget to remove and discard the bouquet garni, or any other whole herbs or spices, such as bay leaves, star anise, and cinnamon sticks.

- If you don't have self-rising flour on hand, you can substitute 1 cup of all-purpose flour, 1½ teaspoons of baking powder, and ½ teaspoon of salt for each 1 cup of self-rising flour called for in the recipe.

white sauce

MAKES ABOUT 2½ cups

2½ cups milk

1 bay leaf

6 black peppercorns

slice of onion

blade of mace

3½ tablespoons butter

⅓ cup plus 1 tablespoon all-purpose flour

salt and pepper

1 Pour the milk into a saucepan and add the bay leaf, peppercorns, onion, and mace.

2 Heat gently to just below boiling point, then remove from the heat, cover, and let steep for 10 minutes.

3 Strain the milk into a heatproof measuring cup or bowl. Melt the butter in a separate saucepan. Sprinkle in the flour and cook over low heat, stirring continuously, for 1 minute.

4 Remove from the heat and gradually stir in the warm milk. Return to the heat and bring to a boil, then cook, stirring, until thickened and smooth. Season with salt and pepper and set aside.

beef stock

MAKES ABOUT 7 CUPS

2¼ pounds beef marrowbones,
    cut into 3-inch pieces

1½ pounds chuck short ribs or
    center cut beef shank, in a single piece

12 cups water

4 cloves

2 onions, halved

2 celery stalks, coarsely chopped

8 black peppercorns

1 bouquet garni (see page 9)

1 Place the bones in a large saucepan and put the meat on top. Add the water and gradually bring to a boil, skimming off the foam that rises to the surface.

2 Press a clove into each onion half and add to the pan with the celery, peppercorns, and bouquet garni. Partly cover and simmer for 3 hours. Remove the meat and simmer for an additional hour.

3 Strain the stock into a bowl, let cool, cover, and store in the refrigerator. When cold, remove and discard the layer of fat from the surface. Use immediately or freeze for up to 6 months.

chicken stock

MAKES ABOUT 10½ CUPS

3 pounds chicken wings and necks

2 onions, cut into wedges

17 cups water

2 carrots, coarsely chopped

2 celery stalks, coarsely chopped

10 fresh parsley sprigs

4 fresh thyme sprigs

2 bay leaves

10 black peppercorns

1 Place the chicken wings and necks and the onions in a stockpot and cook over low heat, stirring frequently, until lightly browned.

2 Add the water and stir well to scrape off any sediment from the bottom of the pot. Gradually bring to a boil, skimming off the foam that rises to the surface. Add all the remaining ingredients, partly cover, and simmer for 3 hours.

3 Strain the stock into a bowl, let cool, cover, and store in the refrigerator. When cold, remove and discard the layer of fat from the surface. Use immediately or freeze for up to 6 months.

fish stock

MAKES ABOUT 5½ CUPS

1½ pounds white fish heads,
  bones, and trimmings, rinsed

1 onion, sliced

2 celery stalks, chopped

1 carrot, sliced

1 bay leaf

4 fresh parsley sprigs

4 black peppercorns

½ lemon, sliced

5½ cups water

½ cup dry white wine

1 Cut out and discard the gills from the fish
heads, then place the heads, bones, and
trimmings in a saucepan.

2 Add all the remaining ingredients and
gradually bring to a boil, skimming off the
foam that rises to the surface. Partly cover and
simmer for 25 minutes.

3 Strain the stock without pressing down on
the contents of the strainer. Let cool, cover,
and store in the refrigerator. Use immediately
or freeze for up to 3 months.

vegetable stock

MAKES ABOUT 5½ CUPS

2 tablespoons sunflower oil

1 onion, finely chopped

½ leek, finely chopped

2 carrots, finely chopped

4 celery stalks, finely chopped

¾ cup finely chopped fennel

1 small tomato, finely chopped

6 cups water

1 bouquet garni (see page 9)

1 Heat the oil in a large saucepan. Add
the onion and leek and cook over low
heat, stirring occasionally, for 5 minutes,
until softened.

2 Add the remaining vegetables and the
tomato, cover, and cook for 10 minutes.
Add the water and bouquet garni, bring to a
boil, and simmer for 20 minutes.

3 Strain the stock into a bowl, let cool,
cover, and store in the refrigerator. Use
immediately or freeze for up to 3 months.

MEAT

01

Beef in Red Wine

SERVES 8

¼ cup all-purpose flour

2¼ pounds lean, boneless beef chuck
  or beef round, diced

8 ounces bacon, diced

¼ cup olive oil

3 tablespoons salted butter

16 pearl onions or shallots

3 garlic cloves, finely chopped

3 cups sliced white button
  mushrooms

2½ cups full-bodied red wine

¾ cup beef stock

bouquet garni (see page 9)

salt and pepper

fresh flat-leaf parsley sprigs,
  to garnish

mashed potatoes, to serve

Method

1 Preheat the oven to 325°F.

2 Season the flour with salt and pepper, and toss the beef in it to coat. Shake off any excess.

3 Heat a large, flameproof casserole dish or Dutch oven, add the bacon, and cook over medium heat, stirring frequently, for 5 minutes, until golden brown. Remove with a slotted spoon. Heat the oil in the casserole dish. Add the beef, in batches, and cook, stirring frequently, for 8–10 minutes, until browned all over. Remove with a slotted spoon.

4 Melt the butter in the casserole dish, then add the onions and garlic and cook, stirring frequently, for 5 minutes, until light golden brown. Add the mushrooms and cook, stirring occasionally, for an additional 5 minutes.

5 Return the beef and bacon to the casserole dish, pour in the wine and stock, add the bouquet garni, and bring to a boil. Cover and transfer the casserole dish to the preheated oven. Cook, stirring two to three times, for 1³/4–2 hours, until the beef is tender. Taste and adjust the seasoning, adding salt and pepper if needed. Remove and discard the bouquet garni. Garnish with parsley sprigs and serve immediately with mashed potatoes.

02

Beef Casserole with Dumplings

SERVES 6

3 tablespoons olive oil

2 onions, finely sliced

2 garlic cloves, chopped

2¼ pounds boneless beef chuck
    or beef round, trimmed and
    cut into strips

2 tablespoons all-purpose flour

1¼ cups beef stock

bouquet garni (see page 9)

⅔ cup red wine

salt and pepper

Herb dumplings

1 cup self-rising flour

¼ cup suet (available from butchers)
    or shortening

1 teaspoon mustard

1 tablespoon chopped fresh parsley,
    plus extra to garnish

1 teaspoon chopped fresh sage

¼ cup cold water

salt and pepper

Method

1 Preheat the oven to 300°F.

2 Heat 1 tablespoon of the oil in a large, flameproof casserole dish or Dutch oven and sauté the onions and garlic until soft and brown. Transfer to a plate.

3 Heat the remaining oil in the casserole dish. Add the beef, in batches, and cook, stirring frequently, for 8–10 minutes, until browned all over.

4 Sprinkle in the flour and stir well. Season well with salt and pepper. Pour in the stock, stirring all the time, then bring to a boil. Return the onions to the casserole dish with the bouquet garni and wine. Cover and bake in the preheated oven for 2–2½ hours.

5 For the dumplings, place the flour, suet, mustard, parsley, and sage in a bowl and season with salt and pepper. Mix well, then add enough of the water to form a firm but soft dough. Break the dough into 12 pieces and roll them into round dumplings.

6 Remove the casserole dish from the oven, discard the bouquet garni, and add the dumplings, pushing them down under the liquid. Cover, return to the oven, and bake for an additional 15 minutes, until the dumplings have doubled in size. Garnish with parsley and serve immediately.

03

Beef Goulash

SERVES 8

¼ cup sunflower oil

2¼ pounds boneless beef chuck or beef round, trimmed and cut into cubes

1 tablespoon all-purpose flour

1 tablespoon paprika, plus extra for sprinkling

2½ cups beef stock

4 tablespoons salted butter

4 onions, chopped

2 carrots, diced

1½ teaspoons caraway seeds

1 teaspoon dried thyme

2 bay leaves

28-ounce can diced tomatoes

2 tablespoons tomato paste

3 potatoes, diced

salt and pepper

sour cream, to serve

Method

1 Preheat the oven to 325°F.

2 Heat the oil in a large skillet. Add the beef, in batches, and cook over medium heat, stirring frequently, for 8–10 minutes, until browned all over. Reduce the heat to low, sprinkle with the flour and paprika, and cook, stirring continuously, for 3–4 minutes. Gradually stir in the stock and bring to a boil, stirring continuously. Remove the skillet from the heat and pour the mixture into a casserole dish or Dutch oven.

3 Melt the butter in the rinsed-out skillet. Add the onions and carrots and cook over low heat, stirring occasionally, for 5 minutes. Add the caraway seeds, thyme, bay leaves, tomatoes, and tomato paste, stir well, and cook for 5 minutes. Add the potatoes, season with salt and pepper, and bring to a boil.

4 Remove the skillet from the heat and pour the mixture into the casserole dish. Stir, cover, transfer to the preheated oven, and cook for 1¾–2 hours, until the meat is tender. Remove from the oven, taste, and adjust the seasoning, adding salt and pepper if needed. Remove and discard the bay leaves. Serve the goulash immediately, topped with a swirl of sour cream and a sprinkling of paprika.

04

Beef & Carrot Stew

SERVES 6

½ cup Thai fish sauce

¼ cup palm sugar or firmly packed
   dark brown sugar

1 teaspoon five-spice powder

4 pounds beef short ribs, or
   3 pounds beef shanks, cut into
   2-inch pieces

3 lemongrass stalks

1 tablespoon vegetable oil

8 large garlic cloves, crushed

6 small–medium shallots, peeled

2-inch piece fresh ginger, thinly
   sliced

5 cups coconut water
   (not coconut milk) or water

2–3 cups water

6 star anise

1 piece cassia bark or cinnamon
   stick, about 4 inches long

4 fresh red Thai chiles or dried red
   Chinese (tien sien) chiles

4 large carrots, peeled and cut
   diagonally into ½-inch-thick
   pieces

salt and pepper

cooked rice, to serve

Method

1 Put the fish sauce and sugar in a large bowl and whisk until the sugar is completely dissolved. Add the five-spice powder and mix well. Add the meat and turn to coat evenly. Transfer the marinade and meat to a plastic food bag and seal the bag. Let marinate in the refrigerator, flipping the bag over every hour or so, for 6 hours.

2 Meanwhile, discard the bruised leaves and root ends of the lemongrass stalks, then halve and crush 6–8 inches of the lower stalks.

3 Heat the oil in a large saucepan over high heat, then add the garlic, shallots, and ginger and stir-fry for 5 minutes, or until golden. Add the coconut water, water, lemongrass, star anise, cassia, and chiles.

4 Reduce the heat to low–medium, add the meat, and marinade with enough water to cover by about 1 inch. Simmer, partly covered, for 2 hours, then add the carrots. Cook for an additional 2–3 hours, or until the meat is tender and falls off the bones. Adjust the seasoning, adding salt and pepper if needed.

5 Skim off any fat from the surface of the stew. Serve immediately with rice.

05

Spicy Beef Casserole

SERVES 4

2 tablespoons all-purpose flour

2 pounds beef chuck or beef round,
   cut into bite-size chunks

2 tablespoons chili oil or olive oil

1 large onion, sliced

1 garlic clove, crushed

1 fresh red chile, seeded and chopped

1 zucchini, sliced

1 red bell pepper, seeded and
   cut into small chunks

2 cups sliced button mushrooms

1 tablespoon tomato paste

2 cups red wine

1 cup beef stock or vegetable stock

1 bay leaf

salt and pepper

Biscuit topping

1⅓ cups self-rising flour, plus
   extra for dusting

2 teaspoons baking powder

pinch of cayenne pepper

pinch of salt

3 tablespoons butter

¼–⅓ cup milk

Method

1 Preheat the oven to 325°F.

2 Put the flour in a bowl and season well with salt and pepper. Add the beef, toss until well coated, and reserve any remaining seasoned flour. Heat half of the oil in a flameproof casserole dish or Dutch oven. Add the beef and cook, stirring, until browned all over. Remove with a slotted spoon. Heat the remaining oil in the casserole dish, add the onion and garlic, and cook over medium heat, stirring, for 2 minutes, until softened. Add the chile, zucchini, red bell pepper, and mushrooms and cook, stirring, for an additional 3 minutes.

3 Stir in the remaining seasoned flour and the tomato paste, then stir in the wine. Pour in the stock, add the bay leaf, then bring to a boil. Reduce the heat and cook over low heat, stirring, until thickened. Return the beef to the casserole dish, cover, and bake in the preheated oven for 45 minutes.

4 Meanwhile, to make the biscuit topping, sift the flour, baking powder, cayenne pepper, and salt into a mixing bowl. Rub in the butter until the mixture resembles fine bread crumbs, then stir in enough of the milk to make a smooth dough. Transfer to a lightly floured work surface, knead lightly, then roll out to a thickness of about ½ inch. Cut out circles using a 2-inch pastry cutter.

5 Remove the casserole dish from the oven and discard the bay leaf. Arrange the dough circles over the top, then return to the oven for an additional 30 minutes, or until the topping is golden brown. Serve immediately.

06

Beef & Olive Casserole

SERVES 6

1¾ pounds beef bottom round
  roast or rump roast, cut into
  1-inch cubes

2 tablespoons olive oil

28-ounce can diced tomatoes

3 cups sliced button mushrooms

strip of finely pared orange rind

2 ounces prosciutto, cut into strips

12 black ripe olives

Marinade

1½ cups dry white wine

2 tablespoons brandy

1 tablespoon white wine vinegar

4 shallots, sliced

4 carrots, sliced

1 garlic clove, finely chopped

6 black peppercorns

4 fresh thyme sprigs

1 fresh rosemary sprig

2 fresh parsley sprigs, plus extra
  to garnish

1 bay leaf

salt

Method

1 Combine the marinade ingredients in a bowl. Add the beef, stirring to coat, then cover with plastic wrap and let stand in the refrigerator to marinate for 8 hours, or overnight.

2 Preheat the oven to 300°F.

3 Drain the beef, reserving the marinade, and pat dry with paper towels. Heat the oil in a large, flameproof casserole dish or Dutch oven. Add the beef, in batches, and cook over medium heat, stirring, for 3–4 minutes, or until browned.

4 Add the tomatoes, mushrooms, and orange rind. Strain the reserved marinade into the casserole dish. Bring to a boil, cover, and bake in the preheated oven for 2½ hours.

5 Remove the casserole dish from the oven, add the ham and olives, and return to the oven for an additional 30 minutes, or until the beef is tender. Discard the orange rind and serve immediately, garnished with parsley sprigs.

07

Rich Beef Casserole

SERVES 2

2 teaspoons vegetable oil

8 ounces extra-lean boneless beef
chuck or beef round, cut into
8 pieces

10 small shallots, peeled but
left whole

1 garlic clove, crushed

1 tomato, chopped

1½ cups finely sliced white button
mushrooms

⅔ cup red wine

½ cup chicken stock

bouquet garni (see page 9)

1 teaspoon cornstarch

salt and pepper

Mustard mashed potatoes

2 starchy potatoes, such as russets
or Yukon gold, sliced

1½ –2 tablespoons skim milk, heated

1 teaspoon Dijon mustard,
or to taste

Method

1 Preheat the oven to 350°F.

2 Heat the oil in a flameproof casserole dish or Dutch oven.
Add the meat and shallots and cook over high heat, stirring,
for 4–5 minutes, or until the meat is browned on all sides. Add
the garlic, tomato, mushrooms, wine, stock, and bouquet garni.
Bring to a simmer, cover, and transfer to the preheated oven
to cook for 45–60 minutes, or until everything is tender.

3 Meanwhile, to make the mustard mashed potatoes, place
the potatoes in a saucepan of boiling water and simmer for
20 minutes, or until just tender. Remove from the heat, drain
well, and return to the saucepan. Add the milk and mash well.
Stir in the mustard and keep warm.

4 Use a slotted spoon to remove the meat and vegetables
from the casserole dish and transfer to a warm serving dish.
Cook the sauce on the stove over high heat until reduced by
half. Reduce the heat, remove the bouquet garni, and adjust
the seasoning, adding salt and pepper if needed.

5 Mix the cornstarch to a paste with a little cold water. Add
to the sauce, stirring well, and bring back to a simmer. Pour
the sauce over the meat and vegetables and serve with the
mustard mashed potatoes.

08

Meatball Stew

SERVES 4

Meatballs

1 bread slice, crusts removed,
   torn into pieces

1½ tablespoons milk

12 ounces fresh ground beef

2 tablespoons chopped fresh parsley,
   plus extra to garnish

1 medium egg

salt and pepper

2 tablespoons olive oil

2 onions, chopped

2 garlic cloves, finely chopped

8 carrots, cut into pieces

5 potatoes, such as white round or
   Yukon gold, cut into pieces

1¼ cups beef stock or water

1 tablespoon sweet paprika

2 cups tomato puree

salt and pepper

Method

1 For the meatballs, place the bread in a bowl with the milk and let soak for 5 minutes. Put the beef, parsley, and egg into a separate bowl. Squeeze out the bread and add it to the bowl, then season with salt and pepper. Mix well until thoroughly combined. Shape the mixture into 16 small balls. Place on a plate, cover, and chill in the refrigerator for 30 minutes.

2 Heat the oil in a large saucepan. Add the meatballs, in batches if necessary, and cook over medium heat, stirring and turning frequently, until browned all over. Remove from the pan and set aside.

3 Add the onions and garlic to the pan and cook over low heat, stirring occasionally, for 5 minutes. Add the carrots and potatoes, then pour in the stock and bring to a boil. Reduce the heat, cover, and simmer for 15 minutes.

4 Add the paprika, stir in the tomato puree, and return the meatballs to the pan. Re-cover the pan and simmer for an additional 15–20 minutes. Season with salt and pepper, garnish with parsley, and serve immediately.

09

Chunky Beef Stew

SERVES 4

1 pound boneless beef chuck
or beef round

1½ tablespoons all-purpose flour

2 tablespoons olive oil

1 onion, chopped

3–4 garlic cloves, crushed

1 fresh green chile, seeded and
chopped

3 celery stalks, sliced

4 whole cloves

1 teaspoon ground allspice

1–2 teaspoons hot pepper sauce,
or to taste

2½ cups beef stock

½ large acorn squash, or other
similar squash, seeded, peeled,
and cut into small chunks

1 large red bell pepper, seeded and
chopped

4 tomatoes, coarsely chopped

10 okra pods, trimmed and halved

cooked rice, to serve

Method

1 Trim any fat or gristle from the beef and cut into 1-inch chunks. Toss the beef in the flour until well coated and reserve any remaining flour.

2 Heat the oil in a large, heavy saucepan and cook the onion, garlic, chile, and celery with the cloves and allspice, stirring frequently, for 3 minutes, or until softened. Add the beef and cook over high heat, stirring frequently, for 3 minutes, or until browned on all sides. Sprinkle in the reserved flour and cook, stirring continuously, for 2 minutes, then remove from the heat.

3 Add the hot pepper sauce and gradually stir in the stock, then return to the heat and bring to a boil, stirring. Reduce the heat, cover, and simmer, stirring occasionally, for 1½ hours.

4 Add the squash and red bell pepper to the saucepan and simmer for 15 minutes. Add the tomatoes and okra and simmer for an additional 15 minutes, or until the beef is tender. Serve immediately with rice.

10

Beef Enchiladas

SERVES 4

Taco sauce

1 tablespoon olive oil

1 onion, finely chopped

1 green bell pepper, seeded and diced

1–2 fresh green chiles, seeded and finely chopped

3 garlic cloves, crushed

1 teaspoon ground cumin

1 teaspoon ground coriander

1 teaspoon light brown sugar

4 tomatoes, peeled and chopped

juice of ½ lemon

salt and pepper

2 tablespoons olive oil, plus extra for brushing

2 large onions, thinly sliced

1¼ pounds lean beef, cut into bite-size pieces

1 tablespoon ground cumin

1–2 teaspoons cayenne pepper

1 teaspoon paprika

8 soft corn tortillas, warmed

2 cups shredded cheddar cheese

salt and pepper

Method

1 Preheat the oven to 350°F. Brush a large casserole dish or other baking dish with oil.

2 To make the sauce, heat the oil in a skillet over medium heat. Add the onion and cook for 5 minutes, or until softened. Stir in the green bell pepper and chiles and cook for 5 minutes. Add the garlic, cumin, coriander, and sugar and cook for an additional 5 minutes, stirring. Stir in the tomatoes and lemon juice and season with salt and pepper. Bring to a boil, then reduce the heat and simmer for 15 minutes.

3 Meanwhile, for the filling, heat the oil in a large skillet over low heat. Add the onions and cook for 10 minutes, or until soft and golden. Remove and set aside.

4 Increase the heat to high, add the beef, and cook, stirring, for 2–3 minutes, or until browned on all sides. Reduce the heat to medium, add the spices, season with salt and pepper, and cook, stirring continuously, for 2 minutes.

5 Divide the beef mixture among the tortillas, top with three-quarters of the cheese, and roll up. Place the tortillas, seam-side down, in the prepared dish, top with the taco sauce and the remaining cheese, and bake in the preheated oven for 30 minutes, or until the topping is golden and bubbling. Serve immediately.

11

Lasagna al Forno

SERVES 4

2 tablespoons olive oil

2 ounces pancetta, chopped

1 onion, chopped

1 garlic clove, finely chopped

8 ounces fresh ground beef

2 celery stalks, chopped

2 carrots, chopped

pinch of sugar

½ teaspoon dried oregano

14½-ounce can diced tomatoes

2 teaspoons Dijon mustard

1¼ cups shredded cheddar cheese or American cheese

1¼ cups white sauce

8 ounces dried oven-ready lasagna noodles

1¼ cups freshly grated Parmesan cheese

salt and pepper

Method

1 Preheat the oven to 375°F.

2 Heat the oil in a large, heavy saucepan. Add the pancetta and cook over medium heat, stirring occasionally, for 3 minutes, or until the fat begins to run. Add the onion and garlic and cook, stirring occasionally, for 5 minutes, or until softened.

3 Add the beef and cook, breaking it up with a wooden spoon, until browned all over. Stir in the celery and carrots and cook for 5 minutes. Season with salt and pepper. Add the sugar, oregano, and tomatoes. Bring to a boil, reduce the heat, and simmer for 30 minutes.

4 Meanwhile, stir the mustard and cheddar cheese into the white sauce.

5 In a rectangular baking dish, make alternate layers of meat sauce, lasagna noodles, and half of the Parmesan cheese. Pour the white sauce over the layers, covering them completely, and sprinkle with the remaining Parmesan cheese. Bake in the preheated oven for 30 minutes, or until golden brown and bubbling. Serve immediately.

12

Lamb & Artichoke Stew

SERVES 4

¼ cup Greek yogurt

grated rind of 1 lemon

2 garlic cloves, crushed

3 tablespoons olive oil

1 teaspoon ground cumin

1½ pounds lean boneless lamb, cubed

1 onion, thinly sliced

⅔ cup dry white wine

5 tomatoes, coarsely chopped

1 tablespoon tomato paste

pinch of sugar

2 tablespoons chopped fresh oregano or 2 teaspoons dried

2 bay leaves

1 cup Kalamata olives

14-ounce can artichoke hearts, drained and halved

salt and pepper

Method

1 Put the yogurt, lemon rind, garlic, 1 tablespoon of the oil, and cumin in a large bowl, season with salt and pepper, and mix together. Add the lamb and toss together until coated in the mixture. Cover and let marinate for at least 1 hour.

2 Heat 1 tablespoon of the remaining oil in a large, heavy saucepan. Add the lamb, in batches, and cook for about 5 minutes, stirring frequently, or until browned on all sides. Using a slotted spoon, remove the meat from the pan. Add the remaining oil to the pan with the onion and sauté for 5 minutes, until softened.

3 Pour the wine into the pan, scraping up any glazed sediment on the bottom of the pan, and bring to a boil. Reduce the heat and return the meat to the pan, then stir in the tomatoes, tomato paste, sugar, oregano, and bay leaves.

4 Cover the pan and simmer for about 1½ hours, or until the lamb is tender. Stir in the olives and artichokes and simmer for an additional 10 minutes. Remove the bay leaves and serve immediately.

13

Lamb & Bell Pepper Casserole

SERVES 4

1 pound lean boneless lamb

1½ tablespoons all-purpose flour

1 teaspoon ground cloves

1–1½ tablespoons olive oil

1 onion, sliced

2–3 garlic cloves, sliced

1¼ cups orange juice

⅔ cup lamb or chicken stock

1 cinnamon stick, bruised

2 red bell peppers, seeded and
   sliced into rings

4 tomatoes

a few fresh cilantro sprigs,
   plus 1 tablespoon chopped fresh
   cilantro, to garnish

salt and pepper

Method

1 Preheat the oven to 375°F.

2 Trim any fat or gristle from the lamb and cut into thin strips. Mix the flour and cloves together. Toss the lamb in the spiced flour until well coated and reserve any remaining spiced flour.

3 Heat 1 tablespoon of the oil in a heavy skillet and cook the lamb over high heat, stirring frequently, for 3 minutes, or until browned on all sides. Transfer to a casserole dish or Dutch oven.

4 Add the onion and garlic to the skillet and cook over medium heat, stirring frequently, for 3 minutes, adding the extra oil if necessary. Sprinkle in the reserved spiced flour and cook, stirring continuously, for 2 minutes, then remove from the heat.

5 Gradually stir in the orange juice and stock, then return to the heat and bring to a boil, stirring. Pour over the lamb in the casserole dish, add the cinnamon stick, red bell peppers, tomatoes, and cilantro, sprigs, and stir well. Cover and cook in the preheated oven for 1½ hours, or until the lamb is tender.

6 Discard the cinnamon stick and season with salt and pepper. Serve immediately, garnished with the chopped cilantro.

14

Lamb Casserole with Almonds

SERVES 4

4 lamb shanks

2 tablespoons olive oil

4 garlic cloves, halved

1 dried chile, crushed

3 fresh rosemary sprigs

6 ripe plum tomatoes

2 large onions, finely chopped

4 strips of orange zest

2 bay leaves

1 teaspoon brown sugar

½ cup red wine

2 cups water

salt and pepper

Almond topping

⅔ cup blanched almonds

2 garlic cloves, finely chopped

grated rind of 2 lemons

small bunch of fresh flat-leaf parsley, chopped

Method

1 Preheat the oven to 350°F. Season the lamb well with salt and pepper. Heat half of the oil in a flameproof casserole dish or Dutch oven. Add the lamb to the casserole dish and brown for 3 minutes on all sides, then remove from the heat. Chop the garlic, chile, and rosemary together.

2 Cut the tomatoes in half and, with the skin side in your hand, grate the flesh to form a coarse tomato pulp. The skin will be left in your hand.

3 Remove the meat from the casserole dish and return the dish to the heat with the remaining oil. Add the garlic, chile, and rosemary and sauté for 2 minutes, until fragrant and aromatic. Add the onions and cook for about 5 minutes, until soft. Season with salt and pepper.

4 Return the meat to the casserole dish with the orange zest, bay leaves, sugar, tomato pulp, wine, and water. Cover and bring to a simmer, then transfer to the preheated oven and cook for 2½ hours, basting regularly.

5 Meanwhile, roast the almonds on a baking sheet in the oven until golden brown. Let cool. When ready to serve, coarsely chop the almonds and place in a bowl with the garlic, lemon rind, and parsley. Mix well. Transfer the lamb shanks to serving plates and sprinkle with a little of the almond topping. Serve immediately.

15

Turkish Lamb Casserole

SERVES 4

2 tablespoons olive oil

4 lamb shanks, about 10½ ounces each

2 onions, sliced

2 bell peppers, any color, seeded and chopped

2 garlic cloves, well crushed

1 eggplant, cut into small cubes

½ teaspoon paprika

½ teaspoon ground cinnamon

1 cup of drained and rinsed, canned chickpeas (garbanzo beans)

14½-ounce canned diced tomatoes

2 teaspoons mixed dried Mediterranean herbs, such as oregano, marjoram, and thyme

½ cup lamb or vegetable stock, plus extra if needed

salt and pepper

cooked couscous, to serve

Method

1 Preheat the oven to 325°F.

2 Heat half of the oil in a large skillet over high heat, add the lamb shanks, and cook, turning frequently, for 2–3 minutes, or until browned all over. Transfer to a casserole dish or Dutch oven.

3 Heat the remaining oil in the skillet over medium-high heat, add the onions and bell peppers, and cook, stirring frequently, for 10–15 minutes, or until soft and just turning golden. Add the garlic, eggplant, and spices and cook, stirring continuously, for 1 minute. Add the chickpeas, tomatoes, herbs, and stock, stir well, and bring to a simmer. Season with salt and pepper and transfer to the casserole dish.

4 Cover the casserole dish, transfer to the preheated oven, and cook for 1½ hours. Check after 45 minutes that the casserole is gently bubbling and that there is enough liquid—if it looks dry, add a little more stock and stir in. Serve immediately with couscous.

16

Mediterranean Lamb Stew

SERVES 4

pinch of saffron threads

2 tablespoons boiling water

1 pound lean boneless lamb

1½ tablespoons all-purpose flour

1 teaspoon ground coriander

½ teaspoon ground cumin

½ teaspoon ground allspice

1 tablespoon olive oil

1 onion, chopped

2–3 garlic cloves, chopped

2 cups lamb stock or chicken stock

1 cinnamon stick, bruised

⅔ cup coarsely chopped
   dried apricots

1 zucchini, sliced

8 cherry tomatoes

1 tablespoon chopped fresh cilantro

salt and pepper

2 tablespoons coarsely chopped
   pistachio nuts, to garnish

cooked couscous, to serve

Method

1 Put the saffron threads in a heatproof bowl with the water and let steep for at least 10 minutes.

2 Trim off any fat or gristle from the lamb and cut into 1-inch chunks. Mix the flour and spices together, then toss the lamb in the spiced flour until well coated and reserve any remaining spiced flour.

3 Heat the oil in a large, heavy saucepan and cook the onion and garlic, stirring frequently, for 5 minutes, or until softened. Add the lamb and cook over high heat, stirring frequently, for 3 minutes, or until browned on all sides. Sprinkle in the reserved spiced flour and cook, stirring continuously, for 2 minutes, then remove from the heat.

4 Gradually stir in the stock and the saffron and its soaking liquid, then return to the heat and bring to a boil, stirring. Add the cinnamon stick and apricots. Reduce the heat, cover, and simmer, stirring occasionally, for 1 hour.

5 Add the zucchini and tomatoes and cook for an additional 15 minutes. Discard the cinnamon stick. Stir in the fresh cilantro and season with salt and pepper. Serve immediately, garnished with the pistachio nuts and accompanied by couscous.

17

Moroccan Lamb Casserole

SERVES 4

1 tablespoon sunflower oil

1 onion, chopped

12 ounces boneless lamb,
  trimmed of all visible fat and
  cut into 1-inch cubes

1 garlic clove, finely chopped

2½ cups vegetable stock

grated rind and juice of 1 orange

1 teaspoon honey

1 cinnamon stick

½-inch piece fresh ginger, finely
  chopped

1 eggplant

4 tomatoes, peeled and chopped

1 cup dried apricots

2 tablespoons chopped fresh cilantro

salt and pepper

cooked couscous, to serve

Method

1 Heat the oil in a large, heavy skillet or a flameproof casserole dish or Dutch oven over medium heat. Add the onion and lamb and cook, stirring frequently, for 5 minutes, or until the meat is lightly browned all over.

2 Add the garlic, stock, orange rind and juice, honey, cinnamon stick, and ginger. Bring to a boil, then reduce the heat, cover, and let simmer for 45 minutes.

3 Using a sharp knife, halve the eggplant lengthwise and slice thinly. Add to the skillet with the tomatoes and apricots. Cover and cook for an additional 45 minutes, or until the lamb is tender.

4 Stir in the cilantro and season with salt and pepper. Serve immediately with couscous.

18

French Country Casserole

SERVES 6

2 tablespoons sunflower oil

4½ pounds boneless leg of lamb,
   cut into 1-inch cubes

6 leeks, sliced

1 tablespoon all-purpose flour

⅔ cup rosé wine

1¼ cups chicken stock

1 tablespoon tomato paste

1 tablespoon sugar

2 tablespoons chopped fresh mint,
   plus extra sprigs to garnish

1 cup dried apricots, chopped

9 potatoes (about 2¼ pounds),
   such as white round, sliced

3 tablespoons unsalted butter,
   melted

salt and pepper

Method

1 Preheat the oven to 350°F.

2 Heat the oil in a large, flameproof casserole dish or Dutch oven. Add the lamb, in batches, and cook over medium heat, stirring, for 5–8 minutes, or until browned all over. Transfer to a plate.

3 Add the leeks to the casserole dish and cook, stirring occasionally, for 5 minutes, or until softened. Sprinkle in the flour and cook, stirring, for 1 minute. Pour in the wine and stock and bring to a boil, stirring. Stir in the tomato paste, sugar, chopped mint, and apricots and season with salt and pepper.

4 Return the lamb to the casserole dish and stir. Arrange the potato slices on top and brush with the melted butter. Cover and bake in the preheated oven for 1½ hours.

5 Increase the oven temperature to 400°F, uncover the casserole dish, and bake for an additional 30 minutes, or until the potato topping is golden brown. Serve immediately, garnished with mint sprigs.

19

Lamb & Chickpea Casserole

SERVES 6

6 tablespoons olive oil

8 ounces chorizo sausage,
  casings removed and cut
  into ¼-inch thick slices

2 large onions, chopped

6 large garlic cloves, crushed

2 pounds boneless leg of lamb,
  cut into 2-inch chunks

1 cup lamb stock or water

½ cup medium-bodied red wine

2 tablespoons sherry vinegar

28-ounce can diced tomatoes

4 fresh thyme sprigs, plus extra
  to garnish

2 bay leaves

½ teaspoon sweet paprika

29-ounce can chickpeas (garbanzo
  beans), drained and rinsed

salt and pepper

Method

1 Preheat the oven to 325°F.

2 Heat ¼ cup of the oil in a large, flameproof casserole dish or Dutch oven over medium-high heat. Reduce the heat, add the chorizo, and cook for 1 minute. Transfer to a plate. Add the onions to the casserole dish and sauté for 2 minutes, then add the garlic and continue cooking for 2 minutes, or until the onions are soft but not brown. Remove from the casserole dish and set aside.

3 Heat the remaining oil in the casserole dish. Add the lamb, in batches if necessary, and cook, stirring, for 5 minutes, until browned on all sides.

4 Return the onion mixture and chorizo to the casserole dish with the lamb. Stir in the stock, wine, vinegar, tomatoes, and salt and pepper. Bring to a boil, scraping any glazed sediments from the bottom of the casserole dish. Reduce the heat and stir in the thyme sprigs, bay leaves, and paprika.

5 Transfer to the preheated oven and cook, covered, for 40–45 minutes, until the lamb is tender. Stir in the chickpeas and return to the oven, uncovered, for 10 minutes.

6 Taste and adjust the seasoning, adding salt and pepper if needed. Serve immediately, garnished with thyme sprigs.

20

Greek Lasagna

SERVES 4

1 tablespoon olive oil

1 onion, chopped

2 garlic cloves, finely chopped

1 pound fresh ground lamb

2 tablespoons tomato paste

2 tablespoons all-purpose flour

1¼ cups chicken stock

1 teaspoon ground cinnamon

4 ounces dried macaroni

2 beefsteak tomatoes, sliced

1¼ cups Greek yogurt

2 eggs, lightly beaten

salt and pepper

salad greens, to serve

Method

1 Preheat the oven to 375°F.

2 Heat the oil in a large, heavy skillet. Add the onion and garlic and cook over low heat, stirring occasionally, for 5 minutes, or until softened. Add the lamb and cook, breaking it up with a wooden spoon, until browned all over.

3 Add the tomato paste and sprinkle in the flour. Cook, stirring, for 1 minute, then stir in the stock. Season with salt and pepper and stir in the cinnamon. Bring to a boil, reduce the heat, cover, and cook for 25 minutes.

4 Meanwhile, bring a large, heavy saucepan of lightly salted water to a boil. Add the pasta, return to a boil, and cook for 8–10 minutes, or according to the package directions, until tender but still firm to the bite.

5 Drain the pasta and stir into the lamb mixture. Spoon into a large casserole dish or other baking dish and arrange the tomato slices on top. Beat together the yogurt and eggs, then spoon over the lamb evenly. Bake in the preheated oven for 1 hour, or until the topping is golden brown. Serve immediately with salad greens.

21

Lamb & Potato Moussaka

SERVES 4

1 large eggplant, sliced

1 tablespoon olive oil

1 onion, finely chopped

1 garlic clove, crushed

12 ounces fresh lean ground lamb

3½ cups sliced white button
   mushrooms

14½-ounce can diced tomatoes
   with herbs

⅔ cup lamb stock

2 tablespoons cornstarch

2 tablespoons water

5 potatoes, parboiled for 10 minutes
   and sliced

2 eggs

½ cup low-fat ricotta cheese

⅔ cup low-fat plain yogurt

½ cup shredded sharp cheddar
   cheese or American cheese

salt and pepper

Method

1 Preheat the oven to 375°F.

2 Lay the eggplant slices on a clean chopping board and sprinkle with salt. Let stand for 10 minutes, then turn the slices over and repeat. Place in a colander, rinse, and drain.

3 Meanwhile, heat the oil in a large saucepan. Add the onion and garlic and cook for 3–4 minutes. Add the lamb and mushrooms and cook over medium heat for 5 minutes, or until browned. Stir in the tomatoes and stock, bring to a boil, and simmer for 10 minutes. Mix the cornstarch and water together to make a smooth paste, then stir into the saucepan. Cook, stirring continuously, until thickened.

4 Spoon half of the mixture into a casserole dish or other baking dish. Cover with the eggplant slices, then the remaining lamb mixture. Arrange the sliced potatoes on top.

5 Beat the eggs, ricotta cheese, and yogurt together. Season with salt and pepper, then pour over the potatoes to cover. Sprinkle with the shredded cheese and bake in the preheated oven for 45 minutes, or until the topping is golden brown. Serve immediately.

22

Pork Stroganoff

SERVES 4

12 ounces lean pork tenderloin

1 tablespoon vegetable oil

1 onion, chopped

2 garlic cloves, crushed

3 tablespoons all-purpose flour

2 tablespoons tomato paste

2 cups chicken stock or
vegetable stock

1¾ cups sliced white button
mushrooms

1 large green bell pepper, seeded and
chopped

½ teaspoon freshly grated nutmeg,
plus extra to garnish

¼ cup low-fat plain yogurt,
plus extra to serve

salt and pepper

chopped fresh parsley, to garnish

cooked rice, to serve

Method

1 Trim off any fat or gristle from the pork and cut into ½-inch thick slices. Heat the oil in a large, heavy skillet and gently cook the pork, onion, and garlic for 4–5 minutes, or until lightly browned.

2 Stir in the flour and tomato paste, then pour in the stock and stir to mix thoroughly. Add the mushrooms, green bell pepper, and nutmeg and season with salt and pepper. Bring to a boil, cover, and simmer for 20 minutes, or until the pork is tender and cooked through.

3 Remove the skillet from the heat and stir in the yogurt. Transfer to warm serving plates. Garnish with parsley and nutmeg and serve immediately with rice and an extra spoonful of yogurt.

23

Pork & Vegetable Stew

SERVES 4

1 pound lean pork tenderloin

1½ tablespoons all-purpose flour

1 teaspoon ground coriander

1 teaspoon ground cumin

1½ teaspoons ground cinnamon

1 tablespoon olive oil

1 onion, chopped

14½-ounce can diced tomatoes

2 tablespoons tomato paste

1¼–2 cups chicken stock

4 carrots, chopped

3 cups peeled, seeded, and chopped
    squash, such as kabocha

2½ leeks, sliced, blanched,
    and drained

10 okra pods, trimmed and sliced

salt and pepper

fresh parsley sprigs, to garnish

cooked couscous, to serve

Method

1 Trim off any fat or gristle from the pork and cut into thin strips about 2 inches long. Mix the flour and spices together. Toss the pork in the spiced flour until well coated and reserve any remaining spiced flour.

2 Heat the oil in a large, heavy saucepan and cook the onion, stirring frequently, for 5 minutes, or until softened. Add the pork and cook over high heat, stirring frequently, for 5 minutes, or until browned on all sides. Sprinkle in the reserved spiced flour and cook, stirring continuously, for 2 minutes, then remove from the heat.

3 Gradually add the tomatoes to the saucepan. Blend the tomato paste with a little of the stock in a bowl or measuring cup and gradually stir into the saucepan, then stir in half of the remaining stock.

4 Add the carrots, then return to the heat and bring to a boil, stirring. Reduce the heat, cover, and simmer, stirring occasionally, for 1½ hours. Add the squash and cook for another 15 minutes.

5 Add the leeks and okra, and the remaining stock if you prefer a thinner stew. Simmer for an additional 15 minutes, or until the pork and vegetables are tender. Season with salt and pepper, garnish with parsley sprigs, and serve immediately with couscous.

24

Pork & White Wine Stew

SERVES 6

⅔ cup all-purpose flour

3 pounds pork tenderloin, cut into
    ½-inch slices

¼ cup sunflower oil

2 onions, thinly sliced

2 garlic cloves, finely chopped

14½-ounce can diced tomatoes

1½ cups dry white wine

1 tablespoon torn fresh basil leaves

2 tablespoons chopped fresh parsley

salt and pepper

fresh oregano sprigs, to garnish

fresh crusty bread, to serve

Method

1 Spread the flour on a plate and season well with salt and
pepper. Coat the pork slices in the flour, shaking off any excess.
Heat the oil in large saucepan. Add the pork slices and cook over
medium heat, turning occasionally, for 4–5 minutes, or until
browned all over. Transfer the pork to a plate with a slotted spoon.
2 Add the onions to the pan and cook over low heat, stirring
occasionally, for 10 minutes, or until golden brown. Add the garlic
and cook for an additional 2 minutes, then add the tomatoes, wine,
and basil and season with salt and pepper. Cook, stirring frequently,
for 3 minutes.
3 Return the pork to the saucepan, cover, and simmer gently for
1 hour, or until the meat is tender. Stir in the parsley, garnish with
oregano sprigs, and serve immediately with crusty bread.

25

Classic French Cassoulet

SERVES 8

2⅔ cups dried cannellini beans,
    soaked overnight or for at least
    5 hours, drained, and rinsed

bouquet garni (see page 9)

1 celery stalk, coarsely chopped

3 onions, 1 quartered, 2 thinly sliced

4 large garlic cloves, 2 whole,
    2 chopped

9 cups water

1¼ pounds pork belly,
    skin removed

2 tablespoons duck fat or
    vegetable oil

1 pound Toulouse sausages or
    other pork sausages

1 pound lamb shoulder, boned and
    cut into 4 large chunks

2 tablespoons tomato paste

3 cups fresh bread crumbs

green salad, to serve

Method

1 Place the beans in a saucepan with enough water to cover, and boil rapidly for 10 minutes. Drain and rinse the beans again, then put them in a large saucepan with the bouquet garni, celery, onion quarters, and whole garlic cloves. Add the 9 cups of water and bring to a boil. Skim off any foam, then reduce the heat to low. Gently simmer for 1 hour, uncovered.

2 Meanwhile, cut the pork belly into 1½-inch pieces, then add the duck fat to a large, heavy saucepan and place over high heat. Add the pork belly and cook until browned all over. Remove and reserve, then repeat with the sausages, then the lamb. Add the sliced onions, chopped garlic, and tomato paste and cook in the remaining fat for 3 minutes. Remove from the heat and let cool.

3 Preheat the oven to 350°F.

4 Drain the beans and set aside, reserving the liquid but discarding the bouquet garni and other vegetables. In a large casserole dish or Dutch oven, layer the beans and meat alternately until they're all used up. Add the onion mixture and enough of the bean-cooking liquid almost to cover. Sprinkle over the bread crumbs, cover, and cook in the preheated oven for 1 hour. Reduce the heat to 275°F, uncover, and cook for an additional hour.

5 Make sure that the cassoulet isn't too dry, adding a little heated bean liquid or water if necessary. Serve immediately with a green salad.

26

Catalan Pork Casserole

SERVES 4–6

2 tablespoons olive oil, plus extra
   if needed

4½ pounds boneless pork shoulder,
   cut into 3-inch chunks

bouquet garni (see page 9)

3¼ cups white wine

3–4 carrots, cut into ½-inch slices

29-ounce can chickpeas (garbanzo
   beans), drained and rinsed

salt and pepper

chopped herbs, to garnish

Sofregit

4 large tomatoes

2 onions, chopped

½ cup olive oil

4 large garlic cloves, finely chopped

1 tablespoon hot paprika

Picada

1 slice day-old country bread

1 tablespoon blanched almonds,
   toasted

1 tablespoon hazelnuts, toasted

2 garlic cloves, crushed

1 ounce semisweet chocolate

olive oil, to create paste

Method

1 For the sofregit, core and halve the tomatoes, then with the skin side in your hand, coarsely grate each tomato halve; discard the cores and skins. Put the onions and oil in a large saucepan and place over medium-high heat. Cook, stirring occasionally, for 10 minutes. Reduce the heat to low and cook for an additional 10–20 minutes, until golden brown. Add the grated tomatoes, garlic, and paprika, and simmer, stirring, for 15 minutes.

2 Preheat the oven to 325°F. Pour the oil into a flameproof casserole dish or Dutch oven and heat over medium-high heat. Brown the pork on all sides in batches, adding more oil if necessary. Pour off any excess fat. Stir in the sofregit, bouquet garni, and salt and pepper. Pour in the wine and enough water to cover, then bring to a boil. Cover and bake in the preheated oven for 1¼ hours. Stir in the carrots, re-cover the casserole dish, and return to the oven for 30 minutes, or until the pork and carrots are tender.

3 Meanwhile, to make the picada, fry the bread in olive oil, let cool, then tear up and put into a food processor. Add the nuts, garlic, and chocolate and process until finely blended. With the motor running, slowly pour in enough oil to form a thick paste.

4 Transfer the casserole dish to the stove. Remove the pork and carrots with a slotted spoon and set aside. Bring the cooking liquid to a boil and place several ladlefuls in a heatproof bowl. Stir in the picada until well blended, then stir this mixture into the casserole dish and boil for 2 minutes. Reduce the heat and add the pork, carrots, and chickpeas. Simmer for about 5 minutes, or until the stew thickens. Serve immediately, garnished with chopped herbs.

27

Pot-Roast Pork

SERVES 4

1 tablespoon sunflower oil

4 tablespoons salted butter

2¼ pounds boneless pork loin, rolled

4 shallots, chopped

6 juniper berries or 1 tablespoon gin

2 fresh thyme sprigs,
   plus extra to garnish

⅔ cup hard dry cider

⅔ cup chicken stock or water

8 celery stalks, chopped

2 tablespoons all-purpose flour

⅔ cup heavy cream

salt and pepper

Method

1 Heat the oil with half of the butter in a large, heavy saucepan. Add the pork and cook over medium heat, turning frequently, for 5–10 minutes, or until browned. Transfer to a plate.

2 Add the shallots to the saucepan and cook, stirring frequently, for 5 minutes, or until softened. Add the juniper berries and thyme sprigs and return the pork to the saucepan with any juices that have collected on the plate. Pour in the cider and stock, season with salt and pepper, then cover and simmer for 30 minutes. Turn the pork over and add the celery. Re-cover the pan and cook for an additional 40 minutes.

3 Meanwhile, make a sauce by mashing the remaining butter with the flour in a small bowl to form a paste. Transfer the pork and celery to a serving plate with a slotted spoon and keep warm. Remove and discard the juniper berries and thyme. Whisk the butter-and-flour paste, a little at a time, into the simmering cooking liquid. Cook, stirring continuously, for 2 minutes, then stir in the cream and bring to a boil.

4 Slice the pork and spoon a little of the sauce over it. Garnish with thyme sprigs and serve immediately. Hand around the remaining sauce separately.

28

Ham & Black-Eyed Pea Stew

SERVES 4

1–1¼ pounds lean cured ham

2½ tablespoons olive oil

1 onion, chopped

2–3 garlic cloves, chopped

2 celery stalks, chopped

3 carrots, sliced

1 cinnamon stick, bruised

½ teaspoon ground cloves

¼ teaspoon freshly grated nutmeg

1 teaspoon dried oregano

2 cups chicken stock or vegetable
    stock

1–2 tablespoons maple syrup

3 large spicy sausages, or
    about 8 ounces chorizo

14–15-ounce can black-eyed peas,
    drained and rinsed

1 orange bell pepper, seeded
    and chopped

1 tablespoon cornstarch

2 tablespoons water

pepper

Method

1 Trim off any fat or skin from the ham and cut into 1½-inch chunks. Heat 1 tablespoon of the oil in a large, heavy saucepan and cook the ham over high heat, stirring frequently, for 5 minutes, or until browned on all sides. Using a slotted spoon, remove from the saucepan and set aside.

2 Add the onion, garlic, celery, and carrots to the saucepan with 1 tablespoon of the remaining oil and cook over medium heat, stirring frequently, for 5 minutes, or until softened. Add the cinnamon, cloves, and nutmeg, season with pepper, and cook, stirring continuously, for 2 minutes.

3 Return the ham to the saucepan. Add the oregano, stock, and maple syrup to taste, then bring to a boil, stirring. Reduce the heat, cover, and simmer, stirring occasionally, for 1 hour.

4 Heat the remaining oil in a skillet and cook the sausages, turning frequently, until browned all over. Remove and cut each into 3–4 chunks, then add to the saucepan. Add the peas and orange bell pepper and simmer for an additional 20 minutes. Blend the cornstarch with the water and stir into the stew, then cook for 3–5 minutes. Serve immediately.

29

Pork & Rice Casserole

SERVES 4

2 tablespoons sunflower oil

2 tablespoons salted butter

1 pound pork tenderloin or pork loin,
   cut into thin strips

1 large onion, chopped

1 red bell pepper, seeded and sliced

1 orange bell pepper, seeded and
   sliced

1⅔ cups sliced white button
   mushrooms

¾ cup long-grain rice

2 cups beef stock

8 ounces smoked sausage, sliced

¼ teaspoon ground allspice

salt and pepper

2 tablespoons chopped fresh parsley,
   to garnish

Method

1 Preheat the oven to 350°F.

2 Heat the oil and butter in a large, flameproof casserole dish or Dutch oven. Add the pork and cook over medium heat, stirring, for 5 minutes, or until browned. Transfer to a plate.

3 Add the onion and cook over low heat, stirring occasionally, for 5 minutes, or until softened. Add the red and orange bell peppers and cook, stirring frequently, for another 4–5 minutes. Add the mushrooms and cook for 1 minute, then stir in the rice. Cook for 1 minute, or until the grains are well coated, then add the stock and bring to a boil.

4 Return the pork to the casserole dish, add the sausage and allspice, and season with salt and pepper. Mix thoroughly, cover, and cook in the preheated oven for 1 hour, or until all the liquid has been absorbed and the meat is tender. Serve immediately, garnished with parsley.

30

Pork & Pasta Casserole

SERVES 4

2 tablespoons olive oil

1 onion, chopped

1 garlic clove, finely chopped

2 carrots, diced

2 ounces pancetta, chopped

1½ cups chopped white button mushrooms

1 pound fresh ground pork

½ cup dry white wine

¼ cup tomato puree

1 cup of canned diced tomatoes

2 teaspoons chopped fresh sage, plus extra sprigs to garnish

8 ounces dried penne

5 ounces mozzarella cheese, diced

¼ cup freshly grated Parmesan cheese

1¼ cups white sauce (see page 9)

salt and pepper

Method

1 Preheat the oven to 400°F.

2 Heat the oil in a large, heavy skillet. Add the onion, garlic, and carrots and cook over low heat, stirring occasionally, for 5 minutes, or until the onion has softened. Add the pancetta and cook for 5 minutes. Add the mushrooms and cook, stirring occasionally, for an additional 2 minutes. Add the pork and cook, breaking it up with a wooden spoon, until the meat is browned all over. Stir in the wine, tomato puree, diced tomatoes, and chopped sage. Season with salt and pepper, bring to a boil, then cover and simmer over low heat for 25–30 minutes.

3 Meanwhile, bring a large, heavy saucepan of lightly salted water to a boil. Add the pasta, return to a boil, and cook for 8–10 minutes, or according to the package directions, until tender but still firm to the bite.

4 Spoon the pork mixture into a large casserole dish or other baking dish. Stir the mozzarella and half of the Parmesan into the white sauce. Drain the pasta and stir into the sauce, then spoon over the pork mixture. Sprinkle with the remaining Parmesan and bake in the preheated oven for 25–30 minutes, or until golden brown. Serve immediately, garnished with sage sprigs.

POULTRY

31

Coq Au Vin

SERVES 4

2 tablespoons salted butter

8 pearl onions

4 ounces bacon, coarsely chopped

4 chicken parts

1 garlic clove, finely chopped

12 white button mushrooms

1¼ cups full-bodied red wine

bouquet garni (see page 9)

1 tablespoon chopped fresh tarragon

2 teaspoons cornstarch

1–2 tablespoons cold water

salt and pepper

chopped fresh flat-leaf parsley,
   to garnish

Method

1 Melt half of the butter in a large skillet over medium heat. Add the onions and bacon and cook, stirring, for 3 minutes. Lift out the bacon and onions and reserve.

2 Melt the remaining butter in the skillet and add the chicken parts. Cook for 3 minutes, then turn over and cook on the other side for 2 minutes. Drain off some of the chicken fat before returning the bacon and onions to the skillet. Add the garlic, mushrooms, wine, bouquet garni, and tarragon. Season with salt and pepper. Cook for about 1 hour, or until the juices run clear when the tip of a sharp knife is inserted into the thickest part of the meat.

3 Remove the skillet from the heat, lift out the chicken, onions, bacon, and mushrooms with a slotted spoon, transfer them to a serving plate, and keep warm. Discard the bouquet garni.

4 Mix the cornstarch with enough of the water to make a paste, then stir into the juices in the skillet. Bring to a boil, reduce the heat, and cook, stirring, for 1 minute. Pour the sauce over the chicken, garnish with parsley, and serve immediately.

32

Chicken Stew with Dumplings

SERVES 4

4 chicken quarters

2 tablespoons sunflower oil

2 leeks, trimmed and sliced

4 carrots, chopped

2 parsnips, chopped

2 small turnips, chopped

2½ cups chicken stock

3 tablespoons Worcestershire sauce

2 fresh rosemary sprigs

salt and pepper

Dumplings

1⅔ cups self-rising flour

½ cup suet (from your local butchers) or shortening

1 tablespoon chopped fresh rosemary leaves

salt and pepper

Method

1 Remove the skin from the chicken if you prefer. Heat the oil in a large, heavy saucepan over medium-high heat and cook the chicken until golden. Using a slotted spoon, remove the chicken from the pan and set aside. Drain off the excess fat.

2 Add the leeks, carrots, parsnips, and turnips to the pan and cook for 5 minutes, until lightly colored. Return the chicken to the pan. Add the stock, Worcestershire sauce, and rosemary sprigs and season with salt and pepper, then bring to a boil. Reduce the heat, cover, and simmer gently for about 50 minutes, or until the juices run clear when the tip of a sharp knife is inserted into the thickest part of the meat.

3 To make the dumplings, add the flour, suet, and chopped rosemary to a bowl, season with salt and pepper, and mix together. Stir in just enough cold water to bind to a firm dough.

4 Form into eight small balls and place on top of the chicken and vegetables. Cover and simmer for an additional 10–12 minutes, until the dumplings are well risen. Serve immediately.

33

Chicken & Tomato Casserole

SERVES 4

1½ tablespoons unsalted butter

2 tablespoons olive oil

1 pound skinless chicken drumsticks

2 red onions, sliced

2 garlic cloves, finely chopped

14½-ounce can diced tomatoes

2 tablespoons chopped fresh flat-
  leaf parsley, plus extra to garnish

6 fresh basil leaves, torn

1 tablespoon sun-dried tomato paste

⅔ cup full-bodied red wine

3 cups sliced white button
  mushrooms

salt and pepper

Method

1 Preheat the oven to 325°F.

2 Heat the butter with the oil in a large, flameproof casserole dish or Dutch oven. Add the chicken drumsticks and cook, turning frequently, for 5–10 minutes, or until browned all over. Using a slotted spoon, transfer the drumsticks to a plate.

3 Add the onions and garlic to the casserole dish and cook over low heat, stirring occasionally, for 10 minutes, or until golden. Add the tomatoes, parsley, basil, sun-dried tomato paste, and wine, and season with salt and pepper. Bring to a boil, then return the chicken drumsticks to the casserole dish, pushing them down under the liquid.

4 Cover and cook in the preheated oven for 50 minutes. Add the mushrooms and cook for an additional 10 minutes, or until the chicken drumsticks are tender and the juices run clear when the tip of a sharp knife is inserted into the thickest part of the meat. Serve immediately, garnished with parsley.

34

Chicken with 40 Garlic Cloves

SERVES 4

3¼–4½-pound chicken

½ lemon

40 whole garlic cloves, peeled

2 tablespoons olive oil

4 fresh thyme sprigs

2 fresh rosemary sprigs

4 fresh parsley sprigs

1 large carrot, coarsely chopped

2 celery stalks, coarsely chopped

1 onion, coarsely chopped

1½ cups white wine

salt and pepper

crusty French bread and a green salad, to serve

Method

1 Preheat the oven to 400°F.

2 Stuff the chicken with the ½ lemon and four of the garlic cloves. Rub the chicken with a little of the oil and some salt and pepper.

3 In a large, flameproof casserole dish or Dutch oven, spread out the remaining garlic cloves, the herbs, carrot, celery, and onion, then place the chicken on top. Pour in the remaining oil and add the wine. Cover with a tight-fitting lid, place in the preheated oven, and bake for 1¼ hours.

4 Remove the chicken from the casserole dish and check that it's cooked by inserting the tip of a sharp knife into the thickest part of the meat; the juices should run clear. Cover and keep warm. Remove the garlic cloves and reserve.

5 Place the casserole dish over low heat and simmer the juices for 5 minutes to make a gravy. Strain, reserving the vegetables.

6 Carve the chicken and serve it with the vegetables from the casserole dish. Squeeze the flesh out of the garlic cloves and spread it on the bread. Serve immediately with the bread and a green salad.

35

Chicken & Barley Stew

SERVES 4

2 tablespoons vegetable oil

8 small skinless chicken thighs

2 cups chicken stock

½ cup pearl barley, rinsed
and drained

6 small new potatoes, scrubbed
and halved lengthwise

2 large carrots, sliced

1 leek, trimmed and sliced

2 shallots, sliced

1 tablespoon tomato paste

1 bay leaf

1 zucchini, trimmed and sliced

2 tablespoons chopped fresh flat-
leaf parsley, plus extra sprigs
to garnish

2 tablespoons all-purpose flour

¼ cup water

salt and pepper

Method

1 Heat the oil in a large saucepan over medium heat. Add the chicken and cook for 3 minutes, then turn over and cook on the other side for an additional 2 minutes. Add the stock, barley, potatoes, carrots, leek, shallots, tomato paste, and bay leaf. Bring to a boil, reduce the heat, and simmer for 30 minutes.

2 Add the zucchini and chopped parsley, cover the pan, and cook for an additional 20 minutes, or until the juices run clear when the tip of a sharp knife is inserted into the thickest part of the meat. Remove the bay leaf and discard.

3 In a separate bowl, mix the flour with the water and stir into a smooth paste. Add it to the pan and cook, stirring, over low heat for an additional 5 minutes. Season with salt and pepper.

4 Remove from the heat, ladle into individual serving bowls, and garnish with parsley sprigs. Serve immediately.

36

Chicken & Pumpkin Casserole

SERVES 4

3 tablespoons olive oil

*5-pound chicken, cut into
    8 pieces and dusted in flour*

*7 ounces fresh chorizo sausages,
    coarsely sliced*

small bunch of fresh sage leaves

1 onion, chopped

6 garlic cloves, sliced

2 celery stalks, sliced

*1 small pumpkin or butternut
    squash, peeled, seeded, and
    coarsely chopped*

1 cup dry sherry

2½ cups chicken stock

14½-ounce can diced tomatoes

2 bay leaves

*1 tablespoon chopped fresh
    flat-leaf parsley*

salt and pepper

Method

1 Preheat the oven to 350°F.

2 Heat the oil in a flameproof casserole dish or Dutch oven and cook the chicken, in batches, with the chorizo and sage leaves, until golden brown. Remove with a slotted spoon and reserve.

3 Add the onion, garlic, celery, and pumpkin to the casserole dish and cook for 20 minutes, or until the mixture is golden brown.

4 Add the sherry, stock, tomatoes, and bay leaves, and season with salt and pepper. Return the reserved chicken, chorizo, and sage to the casserole dish. Cover and cook in the preheated oven for 1 hour.

5 Remove the casserole dish from the oven, stir in the parsley, and serve immediately.

37

Chicken & Squash Casserole

SERVES 4

2 tablespoons olive oil

4 skinless, boneless chicken thighs,
about 4 ounces each, cut
into bite-size pieces

1 large onion, sliced

2 leeks, chopped

2 garlic cloves, chopped

1 butternut squash, peeled,
seeded, and cut into cubes

2 carrots, diced

14½-ounce can diced tomatoes
with herbs

1½ cups of canned mixed beans,
such as pinto beans, black-eyed
peas, and chickpeas (garbanzo
beans), drained and rinsed

½ cup vegetable or chicken stock,
plus extra if needed

salt and pepper

Method

1 Preheat the oven to 325°F.

2 Heat half of the oil in a large, flameproof casserole dish or Dutch oven over high heat, add the chicken, and cook, turning frequently, for 2–3 minutes, until browned all over. Reduce the heat to medium, remove the chicken with a slotted spoon, and set aside.

3 Add the remaining oil to the casserole dish, add the onion and leeks, and cook, stirring occasionally, for 10 minutes, or until soft. Add the garlic, squash, and carrots and cook, stirring, for 2 minutes. Add the tomatoes, beans, and stock, stir well, and bring to a simmer. Return the chicken to the casserole dish.

4 Cover, transfer to the preheated oven, and cook for 1–1¼ hours, stirring once or twice. If the casserole looks too dry, add a little extra stock. Season with salt and pepper and serve immediately.

38

Garlic Chicken Casserole

SERVES 4

¼ cup sunflower oil

2 pounds skinless, boneless chicken breasts, chopped

3½ cups sliced white button mushrooms

16 shallots

6 garlic cloves, crushed

1 tablespoon all-purpose flour

1 cup dry white wine

1 cup chicken stock

bouquet garni (see page 9)

1 celery stalk

14–15-ounce can cranberry (borlotti) beans, drained and rinsed

salt and pepper

steamed squash and crusty bread, to serve

Method

1 Preheat the oven to 300°F.

2 Heat the oil in a flameproof casserole dish or Dutch oven and cook the chicken until browned all over. Using a slotted spoon, remove the chicken from the casserole dish and set aside until required.

3 Add the mushrooms, shallots, and garlic to the casserole dish and cook for 4 minutes. Return the chicken to the dish and sprinkle with the flour, then cook for an additional 2 minutes.

4 Add the wine and stock, stir until boiling, then add the bouquet garni and celery stalk. Season with salt and pepper, then add the cranberry beans.

5 Cover and place in the center of the preheated oven and cook for 2 hours. Discard the bouquet garni and celery stalk and serve the casserole immediately with squash and bread.

39

Chicken Stew with White Wine

SERVES 4–6

2 tablespoons all-purpose flour

3½-pound chicken, cut into
   8 parts, or 8 chicken thighs

4 tablespoons unsalted butter

1 tablespoon sunflower oil

4 shallots, finely chopped

12 white button mushrooms, sliced

2 tablespoons brandy

2 cups white wine

1 cup heavy cream

salt and pepper

chopped fresh flat-leaf parsley,
   to garnish

Method

1 Season the flour with salt and pepper and toss the chicken parts in it to coat. Shake off any excess.

2 Melt 2 tablespoons of the butter with the oil in a large, heavy saucepan over medium-high heat. Add the chicken parts, in batches, and cook, turning frequently, until browned all over. Remove from the pan and set aside.

3 Pour off all the fat and wipe the saucepan with paper towels. Melt the remaining butter in the pan, add the shallots and mushrooms, and sauté, stirring thoroughly, for 3 minutes. Return the chicken to the pan and remove from the heat.

4 Warm the brandy in a small saucepan, ignite, and pour it over the chicken parts to flambé. When the flames die down, return to the heat, pour in the wine, and bring to a boil. Reduce the heat, cover, and simmer for 40–45 minutes, until the chicken is tender and the juices run clear when the tip of a sharp knife is inserted into the thickest part of the meat. Transfer the chicken to a serving plate and keep warm.

5 Skim the fat from the surface of the cooking liquid. Stir in the cream, then bring to a boil and reduce by half. Season with salt and pepper. Spoon the sauce over the chicken parts and garnish with parsley. Serve immediately.

40

Chicken Cacciatore

SERVES 4

1 large chicken

2 tablespoons olive oil

2 ounces pancetta, diced

1 onion, finely chopped

¼ cup white wine

4 tomatoes

1 cup chicken stock

salt and pepper

Method

1 Wash the chicken, pat dry with paper towels, and cut into eight parts. Rub generous amounts of salt and pepper into the skin. Heat the oil in a large, heavy saucepan over medium heat, add the pancetta and onion, and sauté until the onions are translucent.

2 Add the chicken parts and brown on all sides. Deglaze the saucepan with the white wine and let simmer for 5 minutes.

3 Peel and quarter the tomatoes, remove the seeds, and cut into small dice. Add to the chicken, then pour in the stock. Cover and cook over low heat for 30–40 minutes. Season with salt and pepper and serve immediately.

41

Chicken Stew with Apricots

SERVES 4

2 tablespoons olive oil or sunflower
  oil

1 large chicken, cut into 8 parts,
  or 8 chicken thighs

2 large onions, sliced

2 large garlic cloves, crushed

2 teaspoons ground coriander

1½ teaspoons ground ginger

1½ teaspoons ground cumin

pinch of crushed red pepper, to taste
  (optional)

3 cups dried apricots, soaked
  overnight in 1¼ cups orange juice

14 – 15 ounce can chickpeas
  (garbanzo beans), drained
  and rinsed

large pinch of saffron threads

1 preserved lemon, rinsed and sliced

¼ cup slivered almonds, toasted

fresh flat-leaf parsley sprigs,
  to garnish

cooked couscous, to serve

Method

1 Heat the oil in a large, heavy saucepan over medium-high heat.
Add as many chicken parts as will fit without overcrowding and
cook for 3–5 minutes, until golden brown. Remove from the pan
and set aside while you cook the remaining pieces.

2 Pour off all but 2 tablespoons of the oil from the saucepan.
Add the onions and stir for 4 minutes. Add the garlic and continue
stirring for 1–2 minutes, until the onions are soft but not brown.
Stir in the coriander, ginger, cumin, and crushed pepper, if using,
and cook, stirring, for 1 minute.

3 Return the chicken parts to the saucepan with enough water
to cover. Bring to a boil, then reduce the heat and let simmer for
20 minutes. Add the apricots, chickpeas, and saffron and continue
to simmer for 10 minutes, or until the juices run clear when the tip
of a sharp knife is inserted into the thickest part of the chicken.

4 Using a slotted spoon, transfer the chicken, apricots, and
chickpeas to a plate and keep warm. Bring the liquid in the
saucepan to a boil and reduce by half. Pour this liquid over the
chicken, add the preserved lemon, and sprinkle with the slivered
almonds. Transfer to individual plates, garnish with parsley sprigs,
and serve immediately with couscous.

42

Chicken & Apple Casserole

SERVES 4

1 tablespoon olive oil

4 chicken parts, about 5½ ounces each, skinned if preferred

1 onion, chopped

2 celery stalks, coarsely chopped

1½ tablespoons all-purpose flour

1¼ cups apple juice

⅔ cup chicken stock

1 cooking apple, such as Granny Smith, cored and quartered

2 bay leaves

1–2 teaspoons honey

1 yellow bell pepper, seeded and cut into chunks

1 large or 2 medium apples, such as Jonathan or Pink Lady, cored and sliced

1 tablespoon salted butter, melted

2 tablespoons demerara sugar or other raw sugar

salt and pepper

1 tablespoon chopped fresh mint, to garnish

Method

1 Preheat the oven to 375°F.

2 Heat the oil in a deep skillet and cook the chicken over medium-high heat, turning frequently, for 10 minutes, or until browned all over. Using a slotted spoon, transfer to a casserole dish or Dutch oven.

3 Add the onion and celery to the skillet and cook over medium heat, stirring frequently, for 5 minutes, or until softened. Sprinkle in the flour and cook, stirring thoroughly, for 2 minutes, then remove from the heat. Gradually stir in the apple juice and stock, then return to the heat and bring to a boil, stirring. Add the cooking apple, bay leaves, and honey. Season with salt and pepper.

4 Pour this over the chicken in the casserole dish, cover, and cook in the preheated oven for 25 minutes. Add the yellow bell pepper and cook for an additional 10–15 minutes, or until the chicken is tender and the juices run clear when the tip of a sharp knife is inserted into the thickest part of the meat. Remove the bay leaves from the casserole dish.

5 Meanwhile, preheat the broiler to high. Brush the apple slices with half of the butter, sprinkle with half of the sugar, and cook under the broiler for 2–3 minutes, or until the sugar has caramelized. Turn the slices over, brush with the remaining butter, and sprinkle with the remaining sugar, then cook for an additional 2 minutes. Serve the casserole immediately, garnished with the mint and caramelized apple slices.

43

One-Dish Chicken & Rice Stew

SERVES 4

2 tablespoons butter

1 tablespoon sunflower oil

4 large skinless, boneless
  chicken breasts

1 onion, chopped

1 garlic clove, crushed

2 red or green bell peppers, seeded
  and finely chopped

⅓ cup of frozen or canned corn
  kernels, drained if canned

⅓ cup peas

1 bay leaf, torn in half

1 cup dry white wine

1⅓ cups instant long-grain rice

1 cup chicken stock

salt and pepper

chopped fresh parsley,
  to garnish

Method

1 Melt the butter with the oil in a large, heavy saucepan over medium-high heat. Add the chicken breasts, in batches, if necessary, and cook for 3–5 minutes, until golden brown. Remove from the pan and cook the remaining chicken breasts, then remove those from the pan.

2 Pour off all but 1 tablespoon of the oil from the saucepan. Add the onion, garlic, and bell peppers and cook, stirring, for about 5 minutes, until soft but not brown. Return the chicken to the saucepan, add the corn, peas, and bay leaf, then add the wine and let bubble until it has almost all evaporated.

3 Scatter the rice over the chicken breasts, making sure it rests on top of them, then pour in the stock and enough water to cover all the chicken. Season with salt and pepper.

4 Bring to a boil, cover, and reduce the heat to low. Cook for 20 minutes, until all the liquid has been absorbed, the rice is tender, and the juices run clear when the tip of a sharp knife is inserted into the thickest part of the meat.

5 Taste and adjust the seasoning, adding salt and pepper if needed. Garnish with parsley and serve immediately.

44

Herbed Crust Chicken Casserole

SERVES 4

2 tablespoons all-purpose flour

4 chicken legs

1 tablespoon olive oil

1 tablespoon salted butter

1 onion, chopped

3 garlic cloves, sliced

4 parsnips, peeled and cut
  into large chunks

⅔ cup dry white wine

3½ cups chicken stock

3 leeks, white parts only, sliced

½ cup halved prunes (optional)

1 tablespoon English mustard

bouquet garni (see page 9)

2 cups fresh bread crumbs

⅔ cup shredded cheddar cheese

1 cup mixed freshly chopped
  tarragon and flat-leaf parsley

salt and pepper

Method

1 Preheat the oven to 350°F.

2 Season the flour with salt and pepper and toss the chicken in it to coat. Shake off any excess.

3 Heat the oil and butter in a flameproof casserole dish or Dutch oven over medium heat. Add the chicken and cook, turning frequently, until browned all over. Remove with a slotted spoon and keep warm.

4 Add the onion, garlic, and parsnips to the casserole dish and cook for 20 minutes, or until the mixture is golden brown.

5 Add the wine, stock, leeks, prunes (if using), mustard, and bouquet garni. Season with salt and pepper. Return the chicken to the casserole dish, cover, and cook in the preheated oven for 1 hour, or until the juices run clear when the tip of a sharp knife is inserted into the thickest part of the meat. Remove the bouquet garni. Meanwhile, mix together the bread crumbs, cheese, and herbs.

6 Remove the casserole dish from the oven and increase the temperature to 400°F. Uncover the casserole and sprinkle it with the bread crumb mixture. Return to the oven for 10 minutes, uncovered, until the crust starts to brown slightly. Serve immediately.

45

Chicken Casserole

SERVES 4

2 tablespoons all-purpose flour

4 skinless, boneless chicken breasts,
    cut into bite-size chunks

2 tablespoons salted butter

2 tablespoons olive oil

1 large leek, trimmed and sliced

2 scallions, trimmed and chopped

1 garlic clove, crushed

2 carrots, chopped

1 orange bell pepper, seeded
    and chopped

1 tablespoon tomato paste

½ teaspoon ground turmeric

1 cup white wine

1 cup chicken stock

1 bay leaf

salt and pepper

Biscuit topping

1⅓ cups self-rising flour,
    plus extra for dusting

2 teaspoons baking powder

½ teaspoon ground turmeric

pinch of salt

3 tablespoons butter

¼–⅓ cup milk

Method

1 Preheat the oven to 350°F. Put the flour in a bowl and season with salt and pepper. Toss the chicken in the seasoned flour until well coated and reserve any remaining flour.

2 Melt the butter with the oil in a large, flameproof casserole dish or Dutch oven, add the chicken, and cook, stirring, until browned all over. Transfer the chicken to a plate and set aside.

3 Add the leek, scallions, and garlic to the casserole dish and cook over medium heat, stirring, for 2 minutes, until softened. Add the carrots and orange bell pepper and cook for 2 minutes, then stir in the remaining seasoned flour, the tomato paste, and turmeric. Pour in the wine and stock, bring to a boil, then reduce the heat and cook over low heat, stirring, until thickened. Return the chicken to the casserole dish and add the bay leaf. Cover and bake in the preheated oven for 30 minutes.

4 Meanwhile, to make the biscuit topping, sift the flour, baking powder, turmeric, and salt into a mixing bowl. Rub in the butter until the mixture resembles fine bread crumbs, then stir in enough of the milk to make a smooth dough. Transfer to a lightly floured work surface, knead lightly, then roll out to a thickness of about ½ inch. Cut out circles using a 2-inch round pastry cutter.

5 Remove the casserole dish from the oven and discard the bay leaf. Arrange the dough circles over the top, then return to the oven and bake for an additional 30 minutes, or until the topping has risen and is lightly golden. Serve immediately.

46

Leek & Chicken Casserole

SERVES 4

2 waxy potatoes, such as russets or
white round, cubed

7 tablespoons salted butter

1 skinless, boneless chicken breast,
about 6 ounces, cubed

1 leek, sliced

2½ cups sliced cremini mushrooms

2½ tablespoons all-purpose flour

1¼ cups milk

1 tablespoon Dijon mustard

2 tablespoons chopped fresh sage

8 ounces phyllo (filo) pastry,
thawed if frozen

salt and pepper

Method

1 Preheat the oven to 350°F. Cook the potatoes in a saucepan of boiling water for 5 minutes. Drain and set aside.

2 Melt 4½ tablespoons of the butter in a skillet and cook the chicken for 5 minutes, or until browned all over.

3 Add the leek and mushrooms and cook for 3 minutes, stirring. Stir in the flour and cook for 1 minute, stirring thoroughly. Gradually stir in the milk and bring to a boil. Add the mustard, sage, and potatoes, season with salt and pepper, and simmer for 10 minutes.

4 Meanwhile, melt the remaining butter in a small saucepan. Line a deep pie plate with half of the sheets of phyllo pastry. Spoon the chicken mixture into the dish and cover with 1 sheet of pastry. Brush the pastry with a little of the melted butter and lay another sheet on top. Brush this sheet with butter.

5 Cut the remaining phyllo pastry into strips and fold them on top of the pie to create a ruffled effect. Brush the strips with the remaining melted butter and cook in the preheated oven for 45 minutes, or until golden brown and crisp. Serve immediately.

47

Turkey Casserole

SERVES 4

½ cup all-purpose flour

4 turkey breast cutlets

3 tablespoons vegetable oil

1 onion, thinly sliced

1 red bell pepper, seeded and sliced

1¼ cups chicken stock

3 tablespoons raisins

4 tomatoes, peeled, seeded, and
    chopped

1 teaspoon chili powder

½ teaspoon ground cinnamon

pinch of ground cumin

1 ounce semisweet chocolate,
    finely chopped or grated

salt and pepper

fresh cilantro sprigs, to garnish

Method

1 Preheat the oven to 325°F.

2 Spread the flour on a plate and season well with salt and pepper. Coat the turkey cutlets in the seasoned flour, shaking off any excess. Reserve any remaining seasoned flour.

3 Heat the oil in a flameproof casserole dish or Dutch oven. Add the turkey and cook over medium heat, turning occasionally, for 5–10 minutes, or until browned all over. Transfer to a plate with a slotted spoon.

4 Add the onion and red bell pepper to the casserole. Cook over low heat, stirring occasionally, for 5 minutes, or until softened. Sprinkle in the remaining seasoned flour and cook, stirring thoroughly, for 1 minute. Gradually stir in the stock, then add the raisins, tomatoes, chili powder, cinnamon, cumin, and chocolate. Season with salt and pepper. Bring to a boil, stirring thoroughly.

5 Return the turkey to the casserole dish, cover, and cook in the preheated oven for 50 minutes, until cooked through and the juices run clear when the tip of a sharp knife is inserted into the thickest part of the meat. Serve immediately, garnished with cilantro sprigs.

48

Turkey Stew in Piquant Sauce

SERVES 4

2 tablespoons all-purpose flour

2¼ pounds turkey parts

2 tablespoons salted butter

1 tablespoon sunflower oil

2 onions, sliced

1 garlic clove, finely chopped

1 red bell pepper, seeded and sliced

14½-ounce can diced tomatoes

bouquet garni (see page 9)

⅔ cup chicken stock

salt and pepper

2 tablespoons chopped fresh parsley, to garnish

Method

1 Spread the flour on a plate and season well with salt and pepper. Coat the turkey in the seasoned flour, shaking off any excess. Reserve any remaining seasoned flour.

2 Melt the butter with the oil in a large, heavy saucepan. Add the turkey and cook over medium heat, stirring, for 5–10 minutes, or until browned all over. Transfer the turkey pieces to a plate with a slotted spoon and keep warm.

3 Add the onions, garlic, and red bell pepper to the saucepan and cook, stirring occasionally, for 5 minutes, or until soft. Sprinkle in the remaining seasoned flour and cook, stirring thoroughly, for 1 minute.

4 Return the turkey to the saucepan, then add the tomatoes, bouquet garni, and stock. Bring to a boil, stirring thoroughly, then cover and simmer for 1¼ hours, or until cooked through and the juices run clear when the tip of a sharp knife is inserted into the thickest part of the meat.

5 Transfer the turkey to a serving plate with a slotted spoon. Discard the bouquet garni. Return the sauce to a boil and cook until reduced and thickened. Season with salt and pepper and pour the sauce over the turkey. Serve immediately, garnished with parsley.

49

Turkey & Mole Casserole

SERVES 4

4 turkey parts, each cut
  into 4 pieces

about 2 cups chicken stock, plus
  extra for thinning

about 1 cup water

1 onion, chopped

1 whole garlic bulb, divided into
  cloves and peeled

1 celery stalk, chopped

1 bay leaf

1 bunch fresh cilantro, finely
  chopped

1 cup mole sauce
  (use store-bought mole paste,
  thinned as instructed on the
  container)

¼–⅓ cup sesame seeds

Method

1 Preheat the oven to 375°F.

2 Arrange the turkey in a large flameproof casserole or Dutch oven. Pour the stock and water around the turkey, then add the onion, garlic, celery, bay leaf, and half of the cilantro. Cover and bake in the preheated oven for 1–1½ hours, or until the turkey is cooked through and the juices run clear when the tip of a sharp knife is inserted into the thickest part of the meat. Add extra liquid, if needed, and discard the bay leaf.

3 Warm the mole sauce in a saucepan with enough stock to make it the consistency of thin cream.

4 Place the sesame seeds in a dry skillet and dry-fry, shaking the skillet, until lightly golden.

5 Arrange the turkey parts on a serving plate and spoon the warm mole sauce over the top. Sprinkle with the toasted sesame seeds and the remaining chopped cilantro. Serve immediately.

50

Italian Turkey Stew

SERVES 4

1 tablespoon olive oil

4 turkey cutlets

2 red bell peppers, seeded and sliced

1 red onion, sliced

2 garlic cloves, finely chopped

1¼ cups tomato puree

⅔ cup medium white wine

1 tablespoon chopped fresh marjoram

14–15-ounce can cannellini beans, drained and rinsed

3 tablespoons fresh white bread crumbs

salt and pepper

fresh basil sprigs, to garnish

Method

1 Heat the oil in a large ovenproof saucepan, add the turkey, and cook over medium heat for 5–10 minutes, turning occasionally, until browned all over. Transfer to a plate using a slotted spoon.

2 Add the red bell peppers and onion to the saucepan and cook over low heat, stirring occasionally, for 5 minutes, or until softened. Add the garlic and cook for an additional 2 minutes.

3 Return the turkey to the saucepan and add the tomato puree, wine, and marjoram. Season with salt and pepper. Bring to a boil, then reduce the heat, cover, and simmer, stirring occasionally, for 25–30 minutes, or until the turkey is cooked through and tender. Meanwhile, preheat the broiler to medium.

4 Stir the cannellini beans into the saucepan and simmer for an additional 5 minutes. Sprinkle the bread crumbs over the top and place under the preheated broiler for 2–3 minutes, or until golden. Serve immediately, garnished with basil sprigs.

51

Duck & Orange Stew

SERVES 4

1 tablespoon vegetable oil

6 duck legs, 6–8 ounces each, all
  visible fat removed

2 lemongrass stalks

8 large garlic cloves, crushed

1½-inch piece fresh ginger,
  thinly sliced

6 scallions, 4 trimmed and crushed,
  2 trimmed and thinly sliced
  diagonally

4 cups orange juice

juice of 2 limes

¼ cup Thai fish sauce

1 tablespoon palm sugar or
  brown sugar

1 teaspoon five-spice powder

6 star anise

4 fresh red Thai chiles or dried red
  Chinese chiles

2–3 cups water

salt and pepper

cooked rice and lime wedges,
  to serve

Method

1 Heat the oil in a large saucepan over high heat. Add the duck legs and cook for 20 minutes, cooking the first side until crisp and lifting off the bottom of the pan easily, then turning over and cooking the other side.

2 Meanwhile, remove and discard the bruised leaves and root ends of the lemongrass stalks, then halve and crush 6–8 inches of the lower stalks.

3 Transfer the duck legs to a plate using a slotted spoon. Drain off most of the fat from the saucepan, leaving about 1 tablespoon in the pan. Heat over high heat, then add the garlic, ginger, and crushed scallions and stir-fry for 5 minutes, or until fragrant and golden. Add the orange juice, lime juice, fish sauce, sugar, five-spice powder, lemongrass, star anise, and chiles.

4 Reduce the heat to low-medium and return the duck legs to the saucepan. Add enough of the water to cover by about 1 inch. Simmer, partly covered, for 3–4 hours, or until the meat is tender and falling off the bones.

5 Adjust the seasoning, adding salt and pepper if needed. Remove the fat that has risen to the surface with a spoon. Garnish with the sliced scallions and serve with rice and lime wedges.

52

Duck Legs & Olive Stew

SERVES 4

4 duck legs, all visible fat removed

28-ounce can diced tomatoes

8 garlic cloves, peeled but left whole

1 large onion, chopped

1 carrot, finely chopped

1 celery stalk, finely chopped

3 fresh thyme sprigs

10 cup Spanish green olives, stuffed
   with pimentos, garlic, or almonds,
   drained and rinsed

1 teaspoon finely grated orange rind

salt and pepper

Method

1 Put the duck legs in a large, heavy skillet with a tight-fitting lid. Add the tomatoes, garlic, onion, carrot, celery, thyme, and olives and stir together. Season with salt and pepper.

2 Turn the heat to high and cook, uncovered, until the ingredients begin to bubble. Reduce the heat to low, cover tightly, and simmer for 1 1/4–1 1/2 hours, until the duck is tender. Check occasionally and add a little water if the mixture appears to be drying out.

3 When the duck is tender, transfer to a serving plate with a slotted spoon, cover, and keep warm. Leave the casserole dish uncovered, increase the heat to medium, and cook, stirring, for about 10 minutes, until the mixture forms a sauce. Stir in the orange rind, then adjust the seasoning, adding salt and pepper if needed.

4 Mash the tender garlic cloves with a fork and spread over the duck legs. Spoon the sauce over the top. Serve immediately.

53

Duck & Red Wine Stew

SERVES 4

4 duck parts, about 5½ ounces each, all visible fat removed

2 tablespoons olive oil

1 red onion, cut into wedges

2–3 garlic cloves, chopped

1 large carrot, chopped

2 celery stalks, chopped

2 tablespoons all-purpose flour

1¼ cups full-bodied red wine

2 tablespoons brandy (optional)

⅔–1 cup chicken stock or water

3-inch strip of orange rind

2 teaspoons red currant jelly

1 cup sugar snap peas

1⅔ cups white button mushrooms

salt and pepper

1 tablespoon chopped fresh parsley, to garnish

Method

1 Heat a large skillet for 1 minute, until warm but not piping hot. Put the duck parts in the skillet and heat gently until the fat starts to run. Increase the heat a little, then cook, turning over halfway through, for 5 minutes, or until browned on both sides. Transfer to a large saucepan.

2 Add 1 tablespoon of the oil to the skillet and cook the onion, garlic, carrot, and celery, stirring frequently, for 5 minutes, or until softened. Sprinkle in the flour and cook, stirring thoroughly, for 2 minutes, then remove the skillet from the heat.

3 Gradually stir in the wine, brandy, if using, and stock, then return to the heat and bring to a boil, stirring. Season with salt and pepper, then add the orange rind and red currant jelly. Pour the sauce over the duck parts in the large saucepan, cover, and simmer, stirring occasionally, for 1–1¼ hours.

4 Cook the sugar snap peas in a separate saucepan of boiling water for 3 minutes, then drain and add to the stew. Meanwhile, heat the remaining oil in a small saucepan and cook the mushrooms, stirring frequently, for 3 minutes, or until beginning to soften. Add to the stew. Cook the stew for an additional 5 minutes, or until the duck is tender. Serve immediately, garnished with the parsley.

54

Duck Jambalaya Stew

SERVES 4

4 duck breasts, about
 5½ ounces each

2 tablespoons olive oil

8 ounces cured ham,
 cut into small chunks

8 ounces chorizo sausages, outer
 casing removed

1 onion, chopped

3 garlic cloves, chopped

3 celery stalks, chopped

1–2 fresh red chiles, seeded
 and chopped

1 green bell pepper, seeded and
 chopped

2½ cups chicken stock

1 tablespoon chopped fresh oregano

14½-ounce can diced tomatoes

1–2 teaspoons hot pepper sauce,
 or to taste

fresh flat-leaf parsley sprigs,
 to garnish

green salad and cooked rice,
 to serve

Method

1 Remove and discard the skin and any fat from the duck breasts. Cut the flesh into bite-size pieces.

2 Heat half of the oil in a large, deep skillet and cook the duck, ham, and chorizo over high heat, stirring frequently, for 5 minutes, or until browned all over. Using a slotted spoon, remove from the skillet and set aside.

3 Heat the remaining oil in the skillet, then add the onion, garlic, celery, and chiles and cook over medium heat, stirring frequently, for 5 minutes, or until softened. Add the green bell pepper, then stir in the stock, oregano, tomatoes, and hot pepper sauce.

4 Bring to a boil, then reduce the heat and return the duck, ham, and chorizo to the skillet. Cover and simmer, stirring occasionally, for 20 minutes, or until the duck and ham are tender.

5 Serve immediately, garnished with parsley sprigs and accompanied by a green salad and rice.

55

Asian-Inspired Duck Stew

SERVES 4

3 tablespoons soy sauce

½ teaspoon five-spice powder

4 duck legs or breasts,
   cut into pieces

3 tablespoons vegetable oil

1 teaspoon toasted sesame oil

1 teaspoon finely chopped fresh
   ginger

1 large garlic clove, finely chopped

4 scallions, white parts thickly sliced,
   green part shredded

2 tablespoons rice wine or dry sherry

1 tablespoon oyster sauce

3 whole star anise

2 teaspoons black peppercorns

2–2½ cups chicken stock or water

2 tablespoons cornstarch

salt and pepper

Method

1 Combine 1 tablespoon of the soy sauce and the five-spice powder, season with salt and pepper, and rub over the duck pieces. Heat 2½ tablespoons of the vegetable oil in a large, heavy saucepan. Add the duck and cook, turning occasionally, until browned all over. Remove the duck from the saucepan with a slotted spoon and transfer to a plate.

2 Drain the fat from the saucepan and wipe it over with paper towels. Heat the sesame oil and the remaining vegetable oil. Add the ginger and garlic. Cook for a few seconds. Add the sliced white scallions and cook for a few seconds.

3 Return the duck to the saucepan. Add the rice wine, oyster sauce, star anise, peppercorns, and the remaining soy sauce. Pour in enough stock just to cover. Bring to a boil, cover, and simmer gently for 1½ hours, adding more water if needed.

4 Mix the cornstarch with 2 tablespoons of the cooking liquid to a smooth paste. Add to the saucepan, stirring until the sauce has thickened. Garnish with the shredded green scallions and serve immediately.

FISH & SEAFOOD

56

Bouillabaisse

SERVES 8

2¾ pounds sea bass, filleted, skinned, and cut into bite-size chunks

2¾ pounds red snapper, filleted, skinned, and cut into bite-size chunks

3 tablespoons extra virgin olive oil

grated rind of 1 orange

1 garlic clove, finely chopped

pinch of saffron threads

2 tablespoons Pernod

1 pound fresh mussels

1 large cooked crab

1 small fennel bulb, finely chopped

2 celery stalks, finely chopped

1 onion, finely chopped

5 cups fish stock

6 small new potatoes, scrubbed

2 tomatoes, peeled, seeded, and chopped

1 pound large fresh shrimp, peeled and deveined

salt and pepper

Method

1 Put the fish chunks in a large bowl and add 2 tablespoons of the oil, the orange rind, garlic, saffron, and Pernod. Toss the fish pieces until well coated, cover, and let marinate in the refrigerator for 30 minutes.

2 Meanwhile, clean the mussels by scrubbing or scraping the shells and pulling off any beards. Discard any with broken shells and any that refuse to close when tapped. Remove the meat from the crab, chop, and reserve.

3 Heat the remaining oil in a large, heavy casserole and cook the fennel, celery, and onion over low heat, stirring occasionally, for 5 minutes, or until softened. Add the stock and bring to a boil. Add the potatoes and tomatoes and cook over medium heat for 7 minutes.

4 Reduce the heat and add the fish to the stew, beginning with the thickest pieces, then add the mussels, shrimp, and crab and simmer until the fish is opaque, the mussels have opened, and the shrimp have turned pink. Discard any mussels that remain closed. Season with salt and pepper and serve immediately.

57

Spicy Seafood Stew

SERVES 4

4 ounces shrimp, peeled and deveined

8 ounces prepared scallops,
 thawed if frozen

4 ounces monkfish fillet,
 cut into chunks

1 lime, peeled and thinly sliced

1 tablespoon chili powder

1 teaspoon ground cumin

3 tablespoons chopped fresh cilantro

2 garlic cloves, finely chopped

1 fresh green chile, seeded and chopped

2–3 tablespoons vegetable oil

1 onion, coarsely chopped

1 red bell pepper, seeded and
 coarsely chopped

1 yellow bell pepper, seeded and
 coarsely chopped

¼ teaspoon ground cloves

pinch of ground cinnamon

pinch of cayenne pepper

1½ cups fish stock

14½-ounce can diced tomatoes

14–15-ounce can red kidney beans,
 drained and rinsed

salt

Method

1 Place the shrimp, scallops, monkfish, and lime slices in a large, nonmetallic dish with ¼ teaspoon of the chili powder, ¼ teaspoon of the ground cumin, 1 tablespoon of the cilantro, half of the garlic, the chile, and 1 tablespoon of the oil. Cover with plastic wrap and let marinate for up to 1 hour.

2 Meanwhile, heat 1 tablespoon of the remaining oil in a large, heavy saucepan. Add the onion, the remaining garlic, and the red and yellow bell peppers and cook over low heat, stirring occasionally, for 5 minutes, or until softened. Add the remaining chili powder, the remaining cumin, the cloves, cinnamon, and cayenne pepper with the remaining oil, if necessary, and season with salt. Cook, stirring, for 5 minutes, then gradually stir in the stock and tomatoes. Partly cover and simmer for 25 minutes.

3 Add the beans to the saucepan and spoon the fish and shellfish on top. Cover and cook for 10 minutes, or until the fish and shellfish are cooked through. Garnish with the remaining cilantro and serve immediately.

58

Fisherman's Stew

SERVES 6

3¼ pounds fresh mussels

3 tablespoons olive oil

2 onions, chopped

3 garlic cloves, finely chopped

1 red bell pepper, seeded and sliced

3 carrots, chopped

28-ounce can diced tomatoes

½ cup dry white wine

2 tablespoons tomato paste

1 tablespoon chopped fresh dill

2 tablespoons chopped fresh parsley

1 tablespoon chopped fresh thyme

1 tablespoon torn fresh basil leaves, plus extra leaves to garnish

2 pounds white fish fillets, such as cod, flounder, or halibut, cut into chunks

1 pound shrimp, peeled and deveined

1½ cups fish stock or water

salt and pepper

Method

1 Clean the mussels by scrubbing or scraping the shells and pulling off any beards. Discard any with broken shells and any that refuse to close when tapped. Rinse the mussels under cold running water.

2 Heat the oil in a large, heavy saucepan. Add the onions, garlic, red bell pepper, and carrots and cook over low heat, stirring occasionally, for 5 minutes, or until softened.

3 Add the tomatoes, wine, tomato paste, and herbs. Bring to a boil, then reduce the heat and simmer for 20 minutes.

4 Add the fish, mussels, shrimp, and stock and season with salt and pepper. Return the stew to a boil and simmer for 6–8 minutes, or until the shrimp have turned pink and the mussels have opened. Discard any mussels that remain closed.

5 Serve immediately, garnished with basil leaves.

59

Mediterranean Fish Casserole

SERVES 6

2 tablespoons olive oil

1 red onion, sliced

2 garlic cloves, chopped

2 red bell peppers, seeded and
thinly sliced

14½-ounce can diced tomatoes

1 teaspoon chopped fresh oregano
or marjoram

a few saffron strands, soaked in
1 tablespoon warm water for
2 minutes

1 pound white fish fillets, such
as cod, flounder, or halibut,
cut into chunks

1 pound prepared squid,
cut into rings

1¼ cups fish stock or
vegetable stock

4 ounces cooked, peeled shrimp, plus
extra in their shells to garnish

salt and pepper

2 tablespoons chopped fresh parsley,
to garnish

crusty bread, to serve

Method

1 Heat the oil in a skillet and sauté the onion and garlic over medium heat for 2–3 minutes, until beginning to soften.

2 Add the red bell peppers to the skillet and continue to cook over low heat for an additional 5 minutes. Add the tomatoes, oregano, and saffron and stir well.

3 Preheat the oven to 400°F.

4 Place the fish in a large casserole dish or Dutch oven with the squid. Pour in the vegetable mixture and the stock, stir well, and season with salt and pepper.

5 Cover and cook in the preheated oven for about 30 minutes, until the fish is tender and cooked through. Add the shrimp and heat through.

6 Spoon into warm bowls and garnish with the whole shrimp and parsley. Serve immediately with crusty bread to mop up the casserole juices.

60

Spanish Fish Casserole

SERVES 4

¼ cup lemon juice

6 tablespoons olive oil

4 swordfish steaks, about
   6 ounces each

1 onion, finely chopped

1 garlic clove, finely chopped

1 tablespoon all-purpose flour

2 tomatoes, peeled, seeded,
   and chopped

1 tablespoon tomato paste

1¼ cups dry white wine

salt and pepper

fresh dill sprigs, to garnish

crusty bread, to serve

Method

1 Preheat the oven to 350°F.

2 Pour the lemon juice and ¼ cup of the oil in a shallow, nonmetallic dish, stir well, and season with salt and pepper. Add the swordfish steaks, turning to coat thoroughly, then cover with plastic wrap and let marinate in the refrigerator for 1 hour.

3 Heat the remaining oil in a flameproof casserole dish or Dutch oven. Add the onion and cook over low heat, stirring occasionally, for 10 minutes, or until golden. Add the garlic and cook, stirring frequently, for 2 minutes. Sprinkle in the flour and cook, stirring, for 1 minute, then add the tomatoes, tomato paste, and wine. Bring to a boil, stirring.

4 Add the fish to the casserole dish, pushing it under the liquid. Cover and cook in the preheated oven for 20 minutes, or until cooked through and the swordfish flakes easily. Serve immediately with crusty bread, garnished with dill sprigs.

61

Monkfish Ragout

SERVES 4–6

2 tablespoons olive oil

1 small onion, finely chopped

1 red bell pepper, seeded and cut into-inch pieces

1½ cups finely sliced white button mushrooms

3 garlic cloves, very finely chopped

1 tablespoon tomato paste

2 tablespoons chopped fresh flat-leaf parsley

½ teaspoon dried oregano

14½-ounce can diced tomatoes

⅔ cup dry red wine

1¼ pounds monkfish fillets, cut into chunks

1 zucchini, sliced

salt and pepper

6–8 fresh basil leaves, shredded, to garnish

crusty bread, to serve

Method

1 Heat the oil in a heavy saucepan over medium heat. Add the onion, red bell pepper, and mushrooms and cook for 5 minutes, or until beginning to soften.

2 Stir in the garlic, tomato paste, parsley, and oregano. Cook for 1 minute. Pour in the tomatoes and wine. Season with salt and pepper. Bring to a boil, then simmer gently for 10–15 minutes, or until slightly thickened.

3 Add the monkfish and zucchini. Cover and simmer for 15 minutes, or until the monkfish is cooked through and the zucchini is tender but still brightly colored.

4 Garnish with the basil and serve immediately with crusty bread.

62

Seafood Casserole

SERVES 4

1 yellow bell pepper, seeded and
quartered

1 red bell pepper, seeded and
quartered

1 orange bell pepper, seeded and
quartered

45 ripe tomatoes

2 large fresh green chiles

6 garlic cloves, peeled but whole

2 teaspoons dried oregano

2 tablespoons olive oil, plus extra for
drizzling

1 large onion, finely chopped

2 cups fish stock, vegetable stock,
or chicken stock

finely grated rind and juice of 1 lime

2 tablespoons chopped fresh
cilantro, plus extra to garnish

1 bay leaf

1 pound red snapper fillets, skinned
and cut into chunks

8 ounces shrimp, peeled
and deveined

8 ounces squid rings

salt and pepper

warm flour tortillas, to serve

Method

1 Preheat the oven to 400°F.

2 Put the bell pepper quarters, skin-side up, in a roasting pan with the tomatoes, chiles, and garlic. Sprinkle with the oregano and drizzle with oil. Roast in the preheated oven for 30 minutes, or until the bell peppers are well browned and softened.

3 Remove the roasted vegetables from the oven and let stand until cool enough to handle. Peel off the skins from the bell peppers, tomatoes, and chiles and chop the flesh. Finely chop the garlic.

4 Heat the oil in a large saucepan and cook the onion, stirring frequently, for 5 minutes, or until softened. Add the bell peppers, tomatoes, chiles, garlic, stock, lime rind and juice, cilantro, and bay leaf and season with salt and pepper. Bring to a boil, then stir in the fish and seafood. Reduce the heat, cover, and simmer gently for 10 minutes, or until the fish and squid are just cooked through and the shrimp have turned pink.

5 Discard the bay leaf, then garnish with cilantro and serve immediately with flour tortillas.

63

Paella del Mar

SERVES 6

1 pound fresh mussels

6 squid

½ cup olive oil

1 onion, chopped

2 garlic cloves, finely chopped

1 red bell pepper, seeded and
    cut into strips

1 green bell pepper, seeded
    and cut into strips

2 cups risotto rice

2 tomatoes, peeled and chopped

1 tablespoon tomato paste

6 ounces monkfish fillet,
    cut into chunks

6 ounces red snapper fillet,
    cut into chunks

6 ounces cod fillet, cut into chunks

2 cups fish stock

1 cup halved fresh or frozen
    green beans

¾ cup fresh or frozen peas

6 canned artichoke hearts, drained

¼ teaspoon saffron threads

12 jumbo shrimp

salt and pepper

Method

1 Clean the mussels by scrubbing or scraping the shells and pulling off any beards. Discard any with broken shells and any that refuse to close when tapped. Rinse the mussels under cold running water.

2 To prepare each squid, hold the body firmly and grasp the tentacles just inside the body. Pull firmly to remove the innards. Find the transparent quill and remove. Grasp the wings on the outside of the body and pull to remove the outer skin. Trim the tentacles just below the beak and reserve. Wash the body and tentacles under running water. Slice the body into rings. Drain well on paper towels.

3 Heat the oil in a paella pan or large, heavy saucepan. Add the onion, garlic, and bell peppers and cook over medium heat, stirring, for 5 minutes, or until softened. Stir in the prepared squid and cook for 2 minutes. Add the rice and cook, stirring, until transparent and coated with oil.

4 Add the tomatoes, tomato paste, and fish and cook for 3 minutes, then add the stock. Gently stir in the beans, peas, artichoke hearts, and saffron and season with salt and pepper.

5 Arrange the mussels around the edge of the paella pan and top the mixture with the shrimp. Bring to a boil, reduce the heat, and simmer, shaking the pan from time to time, for 15–20 minutes, or until the rice is tender and the shrimp are pink. Discard any mussels that remain closed. Serve immediately.

64

Squid Casserole

SERVES 4

1¾ pounds squid

3 tablespoons olive oil

1 onion, chopped

3 garlic cloves, finely chopped

1 teaspoon chopped fresh
   thyme leaves

14½-ounce can diced tomatoes

⅔ cup red wine

1¼ cups water

1 tablespoon chopped fresh parsley

salt and pepper

crusty bread, to serve

Method

1 Preheat the oven to 275°F.

2 To prepare each squid, hold the body firmly and grasp the tentacles just inside the body. Pull firmly to remove the innards. Find the transparent quill and remove. Grasp the wings on the outside of the body and pull to remove the outer skin. Trim the tentacles just below the beak and reserve. Wash the body and tentacles under running water. Slice the body into rings. Drain well on paper towels.

3 Heat the oil in a large flameproof casserole dish or Dutch oven. Add the prepared squid and cook over medium heat, stirring occasionally, until lightly browned.

4 Reduce the heat and add the onion, garlic, and thyme. Cook, stirring occasionally, for an additional 5 minutes, until softened.

5 Stir in the tomatoes, wine, and water. Bring to a boil, then transfer the casserole dish to the preheated oven for 2 hours. Stir in the parsley and season with salt and pepper. Serve immediately with crusty bread.

65

Seafood & Saffron Stew

SERVES 4

8 ounces fresh mussels

8 ounces fresh clams

2 tablespoons olive oil

1 onion, sliced

pinch of saffron threads

1 tablespoon chopped fresh thyme

2 garlic cloves, finely chopped

28-ounce can diced tomatoes

¾ cup dry white wine

9 cups fish stock

12 ounces red snapper fillets,
    cut into chunks

1 pound monkfish fillets,
    cut into chunks

8 ounces squid rings

2 tablespoons fresh shredded basil
    leaves

salt and pepper

crusty bread, to serve

Method

1 Clean the mussels and clams by scrubbing or scraping the shells and pulling off any beards that are attached to the mussels. Discard any with broken shells and any that refuse to close when tapped.

2 Heat the oil in a large, heavy saucepan and cook the onion with the saffron and thyme over low heat, stirring occasionally, for 5 minutes, or until softened. Add the garlic and cook, stirring, for 2 minutes.

3 Add the tomatoes, wine, and stock, season with salt and pepper, and stir well. Bring to a boil, then reduce the heat and simmer for 15 minutes.

4 Add the fish chunks and simmer for an additional 3 minutes. Add the clams, mussels, and squid rings and simmer for an additional 5 minutes, or until the mussels and clams have opened. Discard any that remain closed. Stir in the basil and serve immediately, accompanied by plenty of crusty bread to mop up the juices.

66

Seafood Gumbo

SERVES 6

2 tablespoons vegetable oil

14 okra pods, trimmed and cut into 1-inch pieces

2 onions, finely chopped

4 celery stalks, finely chopped

1 garlic clove, finely chopped

2 tablespoons all-purpose flour

½ teaspoon sugar

1 teaspoon ground cumin

3 cups fish stock

1 red bell pepper, seeded and chopped

1 green bell pepper, seeded and chopped

2 large tomatoes, chopped

¼ cup chopped fresh parsley

1 tablespoon chopped fresh cilantro

dash of Tabasco sauce

12 ounces cod, halibut, or haddock fillets, skinned and cut into 1-inch chunks

12 ounces monkfish fillets, skinned and cut into 1-inch chunks

12 ounces large shrimp, peeled and deveined

salt and pepper

Method

1 Heat half of the oil in a large, heavy saucepan with a tight-fitting lid and cook the okra over low heat, stirring frequently, for 5 minutes, or until browned. Using a slotted spoon, remove from the pan and set aside.

2 Heat the remaining oil in the saucepan and cook the onion and celery over medium heat, stirring frequently, for 5 minutes, or until softened. Add the garlic and cook, stirring, for 1 minute. Sprinkle in the flour, sugar, and cumin and season with salt and pepper. Cook, stirring thoroughly, for 2 minutes, then remove from the heat.

3 Gradually stir in the stock, then return to the heat and bring to a boil, stirring. Return the okra to the saucepan and add the bell peppers and tomatoes. Partly cover, reduce the heat to low, and simmer gently, stirring occasionally, for 10 minutes.

4 Add the herbs and Tabasco sauce to taste. Gently stir in the fish and shrimp. Cover and simmer gently for 5 minutes, or until the fish is cooked through and the shrimp have turned pink. Transfer to a warm serving dish and serve immediately.

67

Catfish Stew

SERVES 4

2 teaspoons granulated garlic

1 teaspoon celery salt

1 teaspoon pepper

1 teaspoon curry powder

1 teaspoon paprika

pinch of sugar

2 pounds catfish, cut into 4–8 slices

2 tablespoons red wine vinegar

1/3 cup all-purpose flour

6 tablespoons sunflower oil

1 onion, finely chopped

2 garlic cloves, finely chopped

2 tomatoes, chopped

1 fresh marjoram sprig

2½ cups fish stock

¼ teaspoon ground cumin

¼ teaspoon ground cinnamon

2 fresh red or green chiles, seeded and finely chopped

1 each red bell pepper and yellow bell pepper, seeded and finely chopped

salt

parsley sprigs, to garnish

crusty bread, to serve

Method

1 Mix together the granulated garlic, celery salt, pepper, curry powder, paprika, and sugar in a small bowl. Place the fish in a nonmetallic dish and sprinkle with half of the spice mixture. Turn the fish over and sprinkle with the remaining spice mixture. Add the vinegar and turn to coat. Cover with plastic wrap and set aside in the refrigerator to marinate for 1 hour.

2 Spread out the flour in a shallow dish. Drain the fish and dip into the flour to coat, shaking off any excess.

3 Heat 1/4 cup of the oil in a skillet. Add the fish and cook over medium heat for 2–3 minutes on each side. Remove with a spatula and set aside.

4 Wipe the skillet with paper towels, add the remaining oil, and heat. Add the onion and cook over low heat, stirring occasionally, for 5 minutes, until soft. Add the garlic and cook, stirring, for an additional 2 minutes. Add the tomatoes and marjoram, increase the heat to medium, and cook, stirring occasionally, for 8 minutes.

5 Stir in the stock, cumin, and cinnamon and add the fish, chiles, and bell peppers. Bring to a boil, then reduce the heat and simmer for 8–10 minutes, until the fish flakes easily and the sauce has thickened. Season with salt and garnish with parsley sprigs. Serve immediately with crusty bread.

68

French Seafood Stew

SERVES 4–6

large pinch of saffron threads

2 tablespoons olive oil

1 large onion, finely chopped

1 fennel bulb, thinly sliced, green
   tops reserved

2 large garlic cloves, crushed

¼ cup Pernod

4 cups fish stock

2 large ripe tomatoes, peeled,
   seeded, and diced

1 tablespoon tomato paste

1 bay leaf

pinch of sugar

pinch of crushed red peppers
   (optional)

25 large shrimp, peeled and deveined

1 prepared squid, cut into rings

2 pounds firm fish fillets, such as sea
   bass, monkfish, or red snapper, cut
   into large chunks

salt and pepper

Method

1 Put the saffron threads in a small, dry skillet over high heat and toast, stirring thoroughly, for 1 minute. Immediately remove the saffron threads from the skillet and set aside.

2 Heat the oil in a large, heavy saucepan over medium heat. Add the onion and fennel and sauté for 3 minutes, then add the garlic and continue sautéing for an additional 5 minutes, or until the onion and fennel are soft but not colored.

3 Remove the saucepan from the heat. Warm the Pernod in a small saucepan, ignite, and pour it over the onion and fennel to flambé. When the flames have died down, return the saucepan to the heat and stir in the stock, tomatoes, tomato paste, bay leaf, sugar, crushed red pepper, if using, and season with salt and pepper. Slowly bring to a boil, then reduce the heat to low and simmer, uncovered, for 15 minutes.

4 Add the shrimp and squid and simmer until the shrimp turn pink and the squid is opaque. Do not overcook. Discard the bay leaf. Transfer the shrimp and squid to serving bowls and keep warm.

5 Add the fish and the reserved saffron to the saucepan and simmer for 5 minutes, or until the flesh flakes easily. Transfer the fish and broth to the bowls with the shrimp and squid and garnish with the fennel tops. Serve immediately.

69

Moroccan Fish Stew

SERVES 4

2 tablespoons olive oil

1 large onion, finely chopped

pinch of saffron threads

½ teaspoon ground cinnamon

1 teaspoon ground coriander

½ teaspoon ground cumin

1½ teaspoon ground turmeric

1 cup of canned diced tomatoes

1¼ cups fish stock

4 small red snapper fillets

½ cup pitted green olives

1 tablespoon chopped preserved
    lemon

3 tablespoons chopped fresh cilantro

salt and pepper

Method

1 Heat the oil in a heavy saucepan. Add the onion and cook gently over low heat, stirring occasionally, for 10 minutes, or until softened but not colored. Add the saffron, cinnamon, ground coriander, cumin, and turmeric and cook for an additional 30 seconds, stirring thoroughly.

2 Add the tomatoes and stock and stir well. Bring to a boil, reduce the heat, cover, and simmer for 15 minutes. Uncover and simmer for 20–35 minutes, or until thickened.

3 Add the red snapper fillets to the saucepan, pushing them down under the liquid. Let the stew simmer for an additional 5–6 minutes, or until the fish is just cooked.

4 Carefully stir in the olives, preserved lemon, and chopped cilantro. Season with salt and pepper and serve immediately.

70

Seafood with Red Wine Stew

SERVES 4–6

12 ounces fresh mussels

¼ cup olive oil

1 onion, finely chopped

1 green bell pepper, seeded
and chopped

2 garlic cloves, very finely chopped

⅓ cup tomato paste

1 tablespoon chopped fresh
flat-leaf parsley

1 teaspoon dried oregano

14½-ounce can diced tomatoes

1 cup dry red wine

1 pound firm white fish, such
as cod or monkfish, cut into
2-inch pieces

4 ounces prepared scallops, halved

4 ounces shrimp, peeled and
deveined

6-ounce can crabmeat, drained

10–15 fresh basil leaves, shredded

salt and pepper

Method

1 Clean the mussels by scrubbing or scraping the shells and pulling off any beards. Discard any broken shells and any that refuse to close when tapped. Rinse the mussels under cold running water.

2 Heat the oil in a heavy saucepan over medium heat. Add the onion and green bell pepper and cook for 5 minutes, or until beginning to soften.

3 Stir in the garlic, tomato paste, parsley, and oregano and cook for 1 minute, stirring.

4 Pour in the tomatoes and wine. Season with salt and pepper.

5 Bring to a boil, then cover and simmer over low heat for 30 minutes. Add the fish, cover, and simmer for 15 minutes.

6 Add the mussels, scallops, shrimp, and crabmeat. Cover and cook for an additional 15 minutes. Discard any mussels that remain closed. Stir in the basil and serve immediately.

71

Rustic Fish Stew

SERVES 4–6

¼ cup olive oil

1 onion, chopped

2 celery stalks, sliced

3 garlic cloves, sliced

1 tablespoon smoked paprika

small pinch of saffron strands

⅔ cup dry sherry

1½ cups chicken stock or fish stock

2 bay leaves

14½-ounce can diced tomatoes

5 waxy potatoes, such as russets,
    peeled and cut into quarters

2 red bell peppers, seeded and sliced

3¼ pounds mixed fish and seafood,
    such as red snapper, monkfish,
    cod, prepared squid, and shrimp,
    cut into bite-size pieces, and fresh
    mussels (optional)

salt and pepper

chopped fresh parsley and grated
    lemon rind, to garnish

extra virgin olive oil, to serve

Method

1 Heat the olive oil in a large, heavy saucepan and cook the onion, celery, and garlic over medium heat for 2–3 minutes, until beginning to soften.

2 Add the paprika and saffron and cook for an additional minute, then add the sherry and reduce by half.

3 Add the stock, bay leaves, tomatoes, and potatoes, season with salt and pepper, and cook for 10 minutes, or until the potatoes are almost cooked. Add the red bell peppers and cook for an additional 10 minutes.

4 If using fresh mussels, clean them by scrubbing or scraping the shells and pulling off any beards. Discard any with broken shells and any that refuse to close when tapped. Rinse the mussels under cold running water.

5 Carefully add the mussels, if using, and the fish and seafood to the saucepan, stirring only once or twice. Cover and cook for 8–10 minutes, or until the seafood is cooked through. Discard any mussels that remain closed and the bay leaves, turn off the heat, and let stand for 2 minutes.

6 Serve the stew in a large bowl, garnished with parsley and lemon rind. Drizzle with extra virgin olive oil and serve immediately.

72

Squid & Shrimp Stew

SERVES 4

2 tablespoons olive oil

4 scallions, thinly sliced

2 garlic cloves, finely chopped

1¼ pounds prepared squid,
    cut into rings

½ cup dry white wine

1½ cups fresh or frozen fava beans

8 ounces jumbo shrimp,
    peeled and deveined

¼ cup chopped fresh flat-leaf
    parsley

salt and pepper

crusty bread, to serve

Method

1 Heat the oil in a large skillet or heavy saucepan with a lid, add the scallions, and cook over medium heat, stirring occasionally, for 4–5 minutes, until softened. Add the garlic and cook, stirring, for 30 seconds, until softened. Add the squid and cook over high heat, stirring occasionally, for 2 minutes, or until golden brown.

2 Add the wine and bring to a boil. Add the fava beans, then reduce the heat, cover, and simmer for 5–8 minutes if using fresh beans or 4–5 minutes if using frozen beans, until the beans are tender.

3 Add the shrimp and parsley, re-cover, and simmer for an additional 2–3 minutes, until the shrimp have turned pink. Season with salt and pepper. Serve immediately with crusty bread to mop up the juices.

73

Biscuit-Topped Fish Casserole

SERVES 4

2 tablespoons salted butter

2 large leeks, trimmed and sliced

2 cups sliced white button
    mushrooms

2 zucchini, sliced

4 large tomatoes, peeled and
    chopped

1 tablespoon chopped fresh dill

½ cup white wine

1 cup fish stock

4 teaspoons cornstarch

1 pound cod, cut into chunks

salt and pepper

Biscuit topping

1⅓ cups plus 1 tablespoon self-
    rising flour, plus extra for dusting

2 teaspoons baking powder

pinch of salt

1 tablespoon chopped fresh dill

3 tablespoons salted butter

¼–⅓ cup milk

Method

1 Preheat the oven to 400°F.

2 Melt the butter in a large flameproof casserole dish or Dutch oven over low heat. Add the leeks and cook, stirring, for 2 minutes, until slightly softened. Add the mushrooms, zucchini, tomatoes, and dill, and cook, stirring, for an additional 3 minutes.

3 Stir in the wine and stock, bring to a boil, then reduce the heat to a simmer. Mix the cornstarch with a little water to form a paste, then stir it into the casserole dish. Cook, stirring thoroughly, until thickened, then season with salt and pepper and remove from the heat.

4 To make the biscuit topping, sift the flour, baking powder, and salt into a large mixing bowl. Stir in the dill, then rub in the butter until the mixture resembles fine bread crumbs. Stir in enough of the milk to make a smooth dough. Transfer to a lightly floured work surface, knead lightly, then roll out to a thickness of about ½ inch. Cut out circles using a 2-inch round pastry cutter.

5 Add the cod to the casserole dish and stir gently to mix. Arrange the dough circles over the top, then bake in the preheated oven for 30 minutes, or until the biscuit topping has risen and is lightly golden. Serve immediately.

74

Fisherman's Casserole

SERVES 6

2 pounds white fish fillets,
  such as cod, flounder, or
  halibut, skinned

⅔ cup dry white wine

1 tablespoon chopped fresh parsley,
  tarragon or dill

7 tablespoons salted butter, plus
  extra for greasing

2½ cups sliced white button
  mushrooms

6 ounces cooked, peeled shrimp

⅓ cup all-purpose flour

½ cup heavy cream

8 starchy potatoes (about 2 pounds),
  such as white round or Yukon
  gold, cut into chunks

salt and pepper

Method

1 Preheat the oven to 350°F. Grease a medium casserole dish.

2 Fold the fish fillets in half and put in the prepared dish. Season well with salt and pepper, add the wine, and scatter the parsley on top. Cover with aluminum foil and bake in the preheated oven for 15 minutes, until the fish starts to flake. Strain off the liquid and reserve for the sauce. Increase the oven temperature to 425°F.

3 Melt 1 tablspoon of the butter in a skillet over medium heat, add the mushrooms, and cook, stirring frequently, for 5 minutes. Spoon this over the fish. Scatter the shrimp over that.

4 Heat 4 tablespoons of the remaining butter in a saucepan and stir in the flour. Cook for 3–4 minutes without browning, stirring thoroughly. Remove from the heat and gradually add the reserved cooking liquid, stirring well after each addition. Return to the heat and slowly bring to a boil, stirring thoroughly, until thickened. Add the cream and season with salt and pepper. Pour the sauce over the fish in the casserole dish and smooth over the surface.

5 Bring a large saucepan of lightly salted water to a boil, add the potatoes, and cook for 15–20 minutes. Drain well and mash until smooth. Season with salt and pepper, then add the remaining butter, stirring until melted. Pile or pipe the potato onto the fish and sauce and bake for 10–15 minutes, until golden brown. Serve immediately.

75

Macaroni & Seafood Casserole

SERVES 4

12 ounces dried macaroni

3 tablespoons salted butter, plus
  extra for greasing

2 small fennel bulbs, trimmed and
  thinly sliced

2½ cups thinly sliced white button
  mushrooms

6 ounces cooked, peeled shrimp

pinch of cayenne pepper

2½ cups white sauce (see page 9)

⅔ cup freshly grated Parmesan
  cheese

2 large tomatoes, halved and sliced

olive oil, for brushing

1 teaspoon dried oregano

salt

Method

1 Preheat the oven to 350°F. Grease a large casserole dish.

2 Bring a large saucepan of lightly salted water to a boil. Add the pasta, return to a boil, and cook for 8–10 minutes, or according to the package directions, until tender but still firm to the bite. Drain and return to the saucepan. Add 2 tablespoons of the butter to the pasta, cover, shake the saucepan, and keep warm.

3 Melt the remaining butter in a separate saucepan. Add the fennel and cook for 3–4 minutes. Stir in the mushrooms and cook for an additional 2 minutes. Stir in the shrimp, then remove the saucepan from the heat.

4 Stir the cooked pasta, cayenne pepper, and shrimp mixture into the white sauce. Pour the mixture into the prepared dish and spread evenly. Sprinkle with the Parmesan and arrange the tomato slices around the edge. Brush the tomatoes with oil, then sprinkle with the oregano. Bake in the preheated oven for 25 minutes, or until golden brown. Serve immediately.

76

Seafood Lasagna

SERVES 4

3½ tablespoons salted butter, plus extra for greasing

⅓ cup plus 1 tablespoon all-purpose flour

1 teaspoon dry mustard

2½ cups milk

2 tablespoons olive oil

1 onion, chopped

2 garlic cloves, finely chopped

1 pound mixed mushrooms, sliced

⅓ cup white wine

14½-ounce can diced tomatoes

1 pound skinless white fish fillets, such as cod, flounder, or halibut, cut into chunks

8 ounces prepared scallops

4–6 fresh lasagna noodles

8 ounces mozzarella cheese, chopped

salt and pepper

Method

1 Preheat the oven to 400°F. Grease a rectangular baking dish.

2 Melt the butter in a saucepan over low heat. Add the flour and dry mustard and stir until smooth. Simmer gently for 2 minutes, then gradually add the milk, whisking until smooth. Bring to a boil, reduce the heat, and simmer for 2 minutes. Remove from the heat and reserve. Cover the surface of the white sauce with plastic wrap to prevent a skin from forming.

3 Heat the oil in a skillet. Add the onion and garlic and cook gently for 5 minutes, or until softened. Add the mushrooms and cook for 5 minutes, or until softened. Stir in the wine and boil rapidly until almost evaporated, then stir in the tomatoes. Bring to a boil, reduce the heat, and simmer, covered, for 15 minutes. Season with salt and pepper and set aside.

4 Spoon half of the tomato mixture over the bottom of the prepared dish, top with half of the fish and scallops, and layer half the lasagna noodles over the top. Pour over half of the white sauce and sprinkle over half of the mozzarella. Repeat these layers, finishing with the sauce and mozzarella.

5 Bake in the preheated oven for 35–40 minutes, or until golden and the fish is cooked through. Remove from the oven and let stand for 10 minutes before serving.

77

Salmon & Shrimp Casserole

SERVES 6

12 ounces dried spaghetti

5 tablespoons salted butter, plus extra for greasing

7 ounces smoked salmon, cut into strips

10 ounces large cooked, peeled shrimp

1¼ cups white sauce (see page 9)

1⅓ cups freshly grated Parmesan cheese

salt

arugula leaves, to serve

Method

1 Preheat the oven to 350°F. Grease a large casserole dish.

2 Bring a large saucepan of lightly salted water to a boil. Add the pasta, return to a boil, and cook for 8–10 minutes, or according to the package directions, until tender but still firm to the bite. Drain well, return to the saucepan, add 4 tablespoons of the butter, and toss well.

3 Spoon half of the spaghetti into the prepared dish, cover with the smoked salmon, then top with the shrimp. Pour in half of the white sauce and sprinkle with half of the Parmesan. Add the remaining spaghetti, cover with the remaining sauce, and sprinkle with the remaining Parmesan. Dice the remaining butter and dot it over the surface.

4 Bake in the preheated oven for 15 minutes, until the top is golden. Serve immediately with arugula leaves.

78

Tuna Noodle Casserole

SERVES 4–6

7 ounces dried tagliatelle

2 tablespoons salted butter

1 cup fresh bread crumbs

1¾ cups of canned condensed cream of mushroom soup

½ cup milk

2 celery stalks, chopped

1 red bell pepper, seeded and chopped

1 green bell pepper, seeded and chopped

1¼ cups shredded sharp cheddar cheese

2 tablespoons chopped fresh parsley

7 ounces of canned tuna in oil, drained and flaked

salt and pepper

Method

1 Preheat the oven to 400°F.

2 Bring a large saucepan of lightly salted water to a boil. Add the pasta, return to a boil, and cook for 2 minutes less than specified on the package directions. Drain well and set aside.

3 Meanwhile, melt the butter in a separate small saucepan. Stir in the bread crumbs, then remove from the heat and set aside.

4 Pour the soup into a saucepan over medium heat, then stir in the milk, celery, bell peppers, half of the cheese, and the parsley. Add the tuna and stir in gently. Season with salt and pepper. Heat just until small bubbles appear around the edge of the mixture—do not boil.

5 Stir the pasta into the saucepan and use two forks to mix all the ingredients together. Spoon the mixture into an ovenproof dish and spread it out.

6 Stir the remaining cheese into the bread crumb mixture, then sprinkle over the top of the pasta mixture. Bake in the preheated oven for 20–25 minutes, until the topping is golden. Remove from the oven, then let stand for 5 minutes before serving.

4

VEGETABLES
& BEANS

79

Vegetable Casserole

SERVES 8

3½ cups dried cannellini beans, soaked overnight or for at least 5 hours, drained, and rinsed

2 bay leaves

3 onions

4 cloves

1 tablespoon olive oil

4 garlic cloves, finely chopped

4 leeks, sliced

1¾ pounds baby carrots

3 cups white button mushrooms

28-ounce can diced tomatoes

¼ cup chopped fresh parsley

1 tablespoon chopped fresh savory

2½ cups fresh bread crumbs

salt and pepper

Method

1 Put the beans in a saucepan, cover with water, and bring to a rapid boil. Let boil for 10 minutes, then drain and rinse.

2 Return the beans to the rinsed-out saucepan and add the bay leaves. Stud one of the onions with the cloves and add to the pan. Pour in enough water to cover and bring to a boil. Reduce the heat, cover, and simmer for 1 hour, then drain, reserving the cooking liquid. Remove and discard the bay leaves and onion.

3 Preheat the oven to 350°F.

4 Chop the remaining onions. Heat the oil in a flameproof casserole dish or Dutch oven, then add the chopped onions, garlic, and leeks and cook over low heat, stirring occasionally, for 5 minutes, until softened.

5 Add the carrots, mushrooms, and tomatoes, pour in 3½ cups of the reserved cooking liquid, and season with salt and pepper. Bring to a boil, then reduce the heat, cover, and simmer for 15 minutes.

6 Stir in the beans, parsley, and savory and adjust the seasoning, adding salt and pepper if needed. Sprinkle with the bread crumbs and transfer the casserole dish to the preheated oven. Bake, uncovered, for 40–45 minutes, until the topping is golden brown. Serve immediately.

80

Vegetable Stew

SERVES 8

1 red bell pepper, quartered

1 orange bell pepper, quartered

1 green bell pepper, quartered

1 large eggplant, thickly sliced

*2 tablespoons olive oil, plus extra
for brushing*

2 large onions, sliced

3 garlic cloves, finely chopped

3 zucchini, thickly sliced

*8 tomatoes, peeled, seeded,
and chopped*

1½ teaspoons herbes de Provence

2 bay leaves

salt and pepper

crusty bread, to serve

Method

1 Preheat the broiler. Put the bell pepper quarters, skin-side up, on a baking sheet and broil until charred and blistered. Remove with tongs, put them into a plastic food bag, tie the top, and let cool. Meanwhile, spread out the eggplant slices on the baking sheet, brush with oil, and broil for 5 minutes, until lightly browned. Turn, brush with oil, and broil for an additional 5 minutes, until lightly browned. Remove with tongs.

2 Remove the bell peppers from the bag and peel off the skins. Remove and discard the seeds and membranes and cut the flesh into strips. Dice the eggplant slices.

3 Heat the oil in a large saucepan. Add the onions and cook over low heat, stirring occasionally, for 8–10 minutes, until lightly browned. Add the garlic and zucchini and cook, stirring occasionally, for an additional 10 minutes.

4 Stir in the bell peppers, eggplants, tomatoes, herbes de Provence, and bay leaves. Season with salt and pepper, then cover and simmer over low heat, stirring occasionally, for 25 minutes. Remove the lid and simmer, stirring occasionally, for an additional 25–35 minutes, until the vegetables are tender.

5 Remove and discard the bay leaves. Serve the vegetable stew immediately, if serving hot, or let cool, if serving at room temperature, accompanied by crusty bread.

81

Spicy Vegetable Stew

SERVES 4

1 eggplant, cut into 1-inch slices

1 tablespoon olive oil, plus extra
for brushing

1 large red or yellow onion,
finely chopped

2 red or yellow bell peppers, seeded
and finely chopped

3–4 garlic cloves, finely chopped
or crushed

28-ounce can diced tomatoes

1 tablespoon mild chili powder

½ teaspoon ground cumin

½ teaspoon dried oregano

2 small zucchini, quartered
lengthwise and sliced

14–15-ounce can kidney beans,
drained and rinsed

2 cups water

1 tablespoon tomato paste

6 scallions, finely chopped

1 cup shredded cheddar cheese
or American cheese

salt and pepper

crusty bread, to serve

Method

1 Brush the eggplant slices on one side with oil. Heat half of
the oil in a large, heavy skillet. Add the eggplant slices, oiled-
side up, and cook over medium heat for 5–6 minutes, or until
browned on one side. Turn the slices over, cook on the other
side until browned, and transfer to a plate. Cut into bite-size
pieces and set aside.

2 Heat the remaining oil in a large saucepan over medium
heat. Add the onion and bell peppers and cook, stirring
occasionally, for 3–4 minutes, or until the onion is just
softened but not browned. Add the garlic and cook for an
additional 2–3 minutes, or until the onion just begins to color.

3 Add the tomatoes, chili powder, cumin, and oregano. Season
with salt and pepper. Bring just to a boil, reduce the heat,
cover, and simmer gently for 15 minutes.

4 Add the zucchini, eggplant pieces, and kidney beans. Stir in
the water and tomato paste. Return to a boil, then cover the
saucepan and simmer for an additional 45 minutes, or until
the vegetables are tender. Taste and adjust the seasoning,
adding salt and pepper if needed.

5 Ladle into warm bowls and top with the scallions and
cheese. Serve immediately with crusty bread.

82

Tuscan Bean Stew

SERVES 4

1 large fennel bulb

2 tablespoons olive oil

1 red onion, cut into small wedges

2–4 garlic cloves, sliced

1 fresh green chile, seeded and chopped

1 small eggplant, cut into chunks

2 tablespoons tomato paste

2–2½ cups vegetable stock

4 ripe tomatoes

1 tablespoon balsamic vinegar

a few fresh oregano sprigs

14–15-ounce can cranberry (borlotti) beans

14–15-ounce can great Northern beans, drained and rinsed

1 yellow bell pepper, seeded and cut into small strips

1 zucchini, sliced into half moons

½ cup pitted black ripe olives

¼ cup Parmesan cheese shavings

salt and pepper

crusty bread, to serve

Method

1 Trim the fennel and reserve any feathery tops, then cut the bulb into small strips. Heat the oil in a large, heavy saucepan with a tight-fitting lid and cook the onion, garlic, chile, and fennel strips, stirring frequently, for 5–8 minutes, or until softened.

2 Add the eggplant and cook, stirring frequently, for 5 minutes. Blend the tomato paste with a little of the stock and pour into the saucepan. Add the remaining stock, the tomatoes, vinegar, and oregano. Bring to a boil, then reduce the heat, cover, and simmer for 15 minutes, or until the tomatoes have begun to collapse.

3 Add the beans to the saucepan with the yellow bell pepper, zucchini, and olives. Simmer for an additional 15 minutes, or until all the vegetables are tender. Taste and adjust the seasoning, adding salt and pepper if needed. Scatter with the Parmesan shavings and serve immediately, garnished with the reserved fennel tops and accompanied by crusty bread.

83

Italian Vegetable Stew

SERVES 4

4 garlic cloves

1 acorn squash, peeled and seeded

1 red onion, sliced

2 leeks, sliced

1 eggplant, sliced

1 small celeriac, diced

2 turnips, sliced

2 plum tomatoes, chopped

1 carrot, sliced

1 zucchini, sliced

2 red bell peppers, seeded and sliced

1 fennel bulb, sliced

6 ounces Swiss chard

2 bay leaves

½ teaspoon fennel seeds

½ teaspoon chili powder

pinch each of dried thyme, dried
    oregano, and sugar

⅔ cup freshly torn basil leaves

½ cup extra virgin olive oil

1 cup vegetable stock

¼ cup chopped fresh parsley

salt and pepper

2 tablespoons freshly grated
    Parmesan cheese, to serve

Method

1 Finely chop the garlic and dice the squash. Put them in a large, heavy saucepan with all of the other vegetables, the bay leaves, fennel seeds, chili powder, thyme, oregano, sugar, and half of the basil. Pour in the oil and stock. Mix together well, then bring to a boil.

2 Reduce the heat, cover, and simmer for 30 minutes, or until all the vegetables are tender. Discard the bay leaves.

3 Sprinkle in the remaining basil and the parsley and season with salt and pepper. Serve immediately, sprinkled with the Parmesan cheese.

84

Lentil Stew

SERVES 4

1 teaspoon vegetable oil

1 teaspoon crushed garlic

¼ cup finely chopped onion

¼ cup finely chopped leek

¼ cup finely chopped celery

¼ cup seeded and finely chopped green bell pepper

¼ cup finely chopped carrot

¼ cup finely chopped zucchini

1 cup diced flat mushrooms,

¼ cup red wine

pinch of dried thyme

14½-ounce can diced tomatoes, strained through a colander, juice and pulp reserved separately

¼ cup dried green lentils, cooked

2 teaspoon lemon juice

1 teaspoon sugar

¼ cup chopped fresh basil, plus extra to garnish

salt and pepper

cooked spaghetti, to serve

Method

1 Place a large saucepan over low heat, add the oil and garlic, and cook, stirring, until golden brown. Add all the vegetables, except the mushrooms, increase the heat to medium, and cook, stirring occasionally, for 10–12 minutes, or until softened and there is no liquid from the vegetables left in the saucepan.

2 Add the mushrooms and increase the heat to high. Add the wine and cook for 2 minutes, then stir in the thyme and the juice from the tomatoes and cook until reduced by half.

3 Add the lentils, stir in the tomato pulp, and cook for an additional 3–4 minutes. Remove the saucepan from the heat and stir in the lemon juice, sugar, and basil. Season with salt and pepper.

4 Garnish with basil and serve the sauce immediately with the spaghetti.

85

Vegetable & Lentil Casserole

SERVES 4

10 cloves

1 onion, peeled but kept whole

1¼ cups green lentils

1 bay leaf

6½ cups vegetable stock

2 leeks, sliced

2 potatoes, diced

2 carrots, chopped

3 zucchini, sliced

1 celery stalk, chopped

1 red bell pepper, seeded
  and chopped

1 tablespoon lemon juice

salt and pepper

Method

1 Preheat the oven to 350°F.

2 Press the cloves into the onion. Put the lentils into a large casserole dish or Dutch oven, add the onion and bay leaf, and pour in the stock. Cover and cook in the preheated oven for 1 hour.

3 Remove the onion and discard the cloves. Slice the onion and return it to the casserole dish with all the vegetables. Stir thoroughly and season with salt and pepper. Cover and return to the oven for 1 hour.

4 Discard the bay leaf. Stir in the lemon juice and serve immediately.

86

Indian Vegetable Stew

SERVES 4

1 eggplant

2 turnips

8 new potatoes

½ small head cauliflower

3 cups white button mushrooms

1 large onion

3 carrots

⅓ cup ghee or butter

2 garlic cloves, crushed

4 teaspoons chopped fresh ginger

1–2 fresh green chiles, seeded
   and chopped

1 tablespoon paprika

2 teaspoons ground coriander

1 tablespoon curry powder

2 cups vegetable stock

4½-ounce can diced tomatoes

1 green bell pepper, seeded and
   sliced

1 tablespoon cornstarch

⅔ cup coconut milk

2–3 tablespoons ground almonds

salt

fresh cilantro sprigs, to garnish

cooked rice, to serve

Method

1 Cut the eggplant, turnips, and potatoes into ½-inch cubes. Divide the cauliflower into small florets. Leave the button mushrooms whole or slice them thickly, if preferred. Slice the onion and carrots.

2 Heat the ghee in a large, heavy saucepan. Add the onion, turnips, potatoes, and cauliflower and cook over low heat, stirring frequently, for 3 minutes. Add the garlic, ginger, chiles, paprika, ground coriander, and curry powder and cook, stirring, for 1 minute.

3 Add the stock, tomatoes, eggplant, and mushrooms and season with salt. Cover and simmer, stirring occasionally, for 30 minutes, or until the vegetables are tender. Add the green bell pepper and carrots, cover, and cook for an additional 5 minutes.

4 Place the cornstarch and coconut milk in a bowl, mix to form a smooth paste, and stir into the vegetable mixture. Add the ground almonds and simmer, stirring thoroughly, for 2 minutes. Taste and adjust the seasoning, adding salt if needed. Transfer to warm serving plates, garnish with cilantro sprigs, and serve immediately with rice.

87

Spicy Chickpea Stew

SERVES 6

1 tablespoon cumin seeds

2 tablespoons coriander seeds

2 teaspoons dried oregano or thyme

⅓ cup vegetable oil

2 onions, chopped

1 red bell pepper, seeded and cut into ¾-inch chunks

1 eggplant, cut into ¾-inch chunks

2 garlic cloves, chopped

1 fresh green chile, seeded and chopped

14½-ounce can diced tomatoes

14–15-ounce can chickpeas (garbanzo beans), drained and rinsed

2 cups cut green beans (¾-inch pieces)

2½ cups vegetable stock

¼ cup chopped fresh cilantro, plus extra leaves to garnish

Method

1 Dry-fry the seeds in a heavy skillet for a few seconds, until aromatic. Add the oregano and cook for an additional few seconds. Remove from the heat, transfer to a mortar, and crush with a pestle.

2 Heat the oil in a large saucepan. Cook the onions, red bell pepper, and eggplant for 10 minutes, until soft. Add the ground seed mixture, the garlic, and chile, and cook for an additional 2 minutes.

3 Add the tomatoes, chickpeas, green beans, and stock. Bring to a boil, cover, and simmer gently for 1 hour, then stir in the chopped cilantro. Serve immediately, garnished with cilantro leaves.

88

Vegetable Goulash

SERVES 4

¼ cup chopped sun-dried
  tomatoes (not in oil)

1 cup green lentils

2½ cups water

2 tablespoons olive oil

½–1 teaspoon crushed red peppers

2–3 garlic cloves, chopped

1 large onion, cut into small wedges

1 small celeriac, cut into small
  chunks

4 carrots, sliced

6 new potatoes, scrubbed
  and cut into chunks

1 small acorn squash, seeded, peeled,
  and cut into small chunks

2 tablespoons tomato paste

1¼ cups vegetable stock

1–2 teaspoons hot paprika

a few fresh thyme sprigs, plus extra
  to garnish

4 ripe tomatoes

sour cream and crusty bread,
  to serve

Method

1 Put the sun-dried tomatoes in a small heatproof bowl, cover
with almost-boiling water, and let soak for 15–20 minutes. Drain,
reserving the soaking liquid.

2 Meanwhile, rinse and drain the lentils, then put them in a
saucepan with the water and bring to a boil. Reduce the heat,
cover, and simmer for 15 minutes. Drain and set aside.

3 Heat the oil in a large, heavy saucepan with a tight-fitting lid
and cook the chiles, garlic, and vegetables, stirring frequently, for
5–8 minutes, until softened. Blend the tomato paste with a little of
the stock and add to the vegetable mixture, then add the
remaining stock, the lentils, the sun-dried tomatoes and their
soaking liquid, and the paprika and thyme sprigs.

4 Bring to a boil, then reduce the heat, cover, and simmer for
15 minutes. Add the fresh tomatoes and simmer for an additional
15 minutes, or until the vegetables and lentils are tender. Transfer
to warm serving bowls, top with spoonfuls of sour cream, and
garnish with thyme sprigs. Serve immediately with crusty bread.

89

Vegetable Dumpling Stew

SERVES 4

3½ tablespoons salted butter

2 leeks, sliced

2 carrots, sliced

2 potatoes, cut into bite-size pieces

2 sweet potatoes, cut into bite-size pieces

2 zucchini, sliced

1 fennel bulb, halved and sliced

2 tablespoons all-purpose flour

15–16-ounce can lima beans, drained and rinsed, with liquid reserved

2 cups vegetable stock

2 tablespoons tomato paste

1 teaspoon dried thyme

2 bay leaves

salt and pepper

Dumplings

1 cup self-rising flour

pinch of salt

¼ cup vegetable shortening

2 tablespoons chopped fresh parsley

¼ cup water

Method

1 Melt the butter in a large saucepan over low heat. Add the leeks, carrots, potatoes, sweet potatoes, zucchini, and fennel and cook, stirring occasionally, for 10 minutes. Stir in the flour and cook, stirring thoroughly, for 1 minute. Stir in the can juices from the beans, the stock, tomato paste, thyme, and bay leaves. Season with salt and pepper. Bring to a boil, stirring thoroughly, then cover and simmer for 10 minutes.

2 To make the dumplings, sift the flour and salt into a mixing bowl, add the shortening, and mix well. Stir in the parsley and then pour in enough of the water to form a firm but soft dough. Break the dough into eight pieces and roll them into round dumplings.

3 Add the lima beans and the dumplings to the pan, pushing them under the liquid. Cover and simmer for an additional 30 minutes, or until the dumplings have doubled in size.

4 Remove and discard the bay leaves and serve the stew and dumplings immediately.

90

Lentil & Rice Stew

SERVES 4

1 cup red lentils

⅓ cup long-grain rice

5 cups vegetable stock

1 leek, cut into chunks

3 garlic cloves, crushed

14½-ounce can diced tomatoes

1 teaspoon ground cumin

1 teaspoon chili powder

1 teaspoon garam masala

1 red bell pepper, seeded and sliced

1½ cups small broccoli florets

8 baby ears of corn, halved
  lengthwise

½ cup halved green beans

1 tablespoon shredded fresh basil,
  plus extra sprigs to garnish

salt and pepper

Method

1 Place the lentils, rice, and stock in a large, heavy saucepan and cook over low heat, stirring occasionally, for 20 minutes.

2 Add the leek, garlic, tomatoes, cumin, chili powder, garam masala, red bell pepper, broccoli, baby ears of corn, and green beans to the saucepan.

3 Bring to a boil, then reduce the heat, cover, and simmer for 10–15 minutes, or until the vegetables are tender.

4 Add the shredded basil and season with salt and pepper.

5 Garnish with basil sprigs and serve immediately.

91

Squash & Vegetable Casserole

SERVES 4–6

1 onion, sliced

2 leeks, sliced

2 celery stalks, chopped

2 carrots, thinly sliced

1 red bell pepper, seeded and sliced

2 cups diced butternut squash
   or pumpkin

2 parsnips, diced

1 large sweet potato, diced

14½-ounce can diced tomatoes

⅔–1 cup hard dry cider

2 teaspoons herbes de Provence

salt and pepper

fresh flat-leaf parsley leaves,
   to garnish

Method

1 Preheat the oven to 350°F.

2 Place the onion, leeks, celery, carrots, red bell pepper, squash, parsnips, and sweet potatoes in a large casserole dish or Dutch oven and mix well. Stir in the tomatoes, ⅔ cup of the cider, and the herbes de Provence. Season with salt and pepper.

3 Cover and bake in the preheated oven, stirring once or twice and adding a little extra cider if needed, for 1¼–1½ hours, or until the vegetables are cooked through and tender. Serve immediately, garnished with parsley leaves.

92

Fresh Vegetable Stew

SERVES 4

1¼ cups dried cannellini beans,
   soaked overnight or for at least
   5 hours and drained

2 tablespoons olive oil

4–8 pearl onions, halved

2 celery stalks, cut into
   ¼-inch slices

8 ounces baby carrots, scrubbed
   and halved if large

8 new potatoes, scrubbed and
   halved or quartered if large

3½–5 cups vegetable stock

bouquet garni (see page 9)

1½–2 tablespoons light soy sauce

6 baby ears of corn

¾ cup shelled fava beans, thawed
   if frozen

½–1 savoy or green cabbage
   (about 8 ounces)

1½ tablespoons cornstarch

2 tablespoons cold water

salt and pepper

½–1 cup grated Parmesan cheese,
   to serve

Method

1 Put the beans in a large saucepan, add water to cover, and bring to a boil. Boil the beans rapidly for 20 minutes, then drain and set aside.

2 Heat the oil in a large, heavy saucepan with a tight-fitting lid, add the onions, celery, carrots, and potatoes, and cook, stirring frequently, for 5 minutes, or until softened. Add the stock, drained beans, bouquet garni, and soy sauce, then bring to a boil. Reduce the heat, cover, and simmer for 12 minutes.

3 Add the baby ears of corn and fava beans and season with salt and pepper. Simmer for an additional 3 minutes.

4 Meanwhile, discard the outer leaves and hard middle core from the cabbage and shred the leaves. Add to the saucepan and simmer for an additional 3–5 minutes, or until all the vegetables are tender.

5 Blend the cornstarch with the water, stir into the saucepan, and cook, stirring, for 4–6 minutes, or until the liquid has thickened. Discard the bouquet garni. Spoon into warm bowls and sprinkle with the cheese. Serve immediately.

93

Bean & Pasta Casserole

SERVES 4

1¼ cups dried cannellini beans,
    soaked overnight or for at least
    5 hours, drained, and rinsed

8 ounces dried penne

6 tablespoons olive oil

3½ cups vegetable stock

2 large onions, sliced

2 garlic cloves, chopped

2 bay leaves

1 teaspoon dried oregano

1 teaspoon dried thyme

⅓ cup red wine

2 tablespoons tomato paste

2 celery stalks, sliced

1 fennel bulb, sliced

1½ cups sliced white button
    mushrooms

2 tomatoes, sliced

1 teaspoon dark brown sugar

1 cup dry white bread crumbs

salt and pepper

crusty bread, to serve

Method

1 Preheat the oven to 350°F.

2 Put the beans in a large saucepan, add water to cover, and bring to a boil. Boil the beans rapidly for 20 minutes, then drain and set aside.

3 Cook the pasta in a large saucepan of boiling salted water, adding 1 tablespoon of the oil, for 3 minutes. Drain and set aside.

4 Put the beans in a large, flameproof casserole dish or Dutch oven and pour in the stock, then stir in the remaining oil, the onions, garlic, bay leaves, herbs, wine, and tomato paste. Bring to a boil, cover, and cook in the preheated oven for 2 hours.

5 Remove the casserole dish from the oven and discard the bay leaves. Add the reserved pasta, the celery, fennel, mushrooms, and tomatoes and season with salt and pepper. Stir in the sugar and sprinkle the bread crumbs on top. Cover, return to the oven, and continue cooking for 1 hour. Serve immediately with crusty bread.

94

Mixed Bean Casserole

SERVES 4

1 large onion, chopped

½ cup of drained and rinsed
canned red kidney beans

½ cup of drained and rinsed
canned lima beans

½ cup of drained and rinsed canned
chickpeas (garbanzo beans)

2 zucchini, coarsely chopped

2 large carrots, coarsely chopped

4 tomatoes, peeled and coarsely
chopped

2 celery stalks, chopped

1¼ cups vegetable stock

2 tablespoons tomato paste

salt and pepper

Crisp topping

2 cups whole-wheat bread crumbs

¼ cup finely chopped hazelnuts

1 tablespoon chopped fresh parsley

1 cup shredded American cheese or
cheddar cheese

Method

1 Preheat the oven to 350°F.

2 Put the onion, kidney beans, lima beans, chickpeas, zucchini, carrots, tomatoes, and celery in a large, casserole dish or Dutch oven. Mix together the stock and tomato paste and pour this over the vegetables. Season with salt and pepper. Transfer to the preheated oven and bake for 15 minutes.

3 Meanwhile, to make the crisp topping, put the bread crumbs in a large bowl, add the hazelnuts, parsley, and cheese and mix together well.

4 Remove the vegetables from the oven and carefully sprinkle with the topping. Do not press down or it will sink into the vegetables and turn mushy.

5 Return the casserole dish to the oven and bake for 30 minutes, or until the crisp topping is golden brown. Remove from the oven and serve immediately.

95

Spicy Vegetable Casserole

SERVES 4

1 large onion, sliced

2 zucchini, sliced

1 cup sliced white button
   mushrooms

2 large carrots, coarsely chopped

1 cup of drained and rinsed canned
   black-eyed peas

¾ cup of drained and rinsed canned
   cannellini beans

14½-ounce can diced tomatoes

1 teaspoon mild chili powder

salt and pepper

Biscuit topping

1⅓ cup plus 1 tablespoon self-rising
   flour, plus extra for dusting

2 teaspoons baking powder

½ teaspoon paprika

pinch of salt

3 tablespoons unsalted butter

¼–⅓ cup milk

Method

1 Preheat the oven to 400°F.

2 Put the onion, zucchini, mushrooms, carrots, black-eyed peas, cannellini beans, and tomatoes in a casserole dish or Dutch oven. Sprinkle with the chili powder and season with salt and pepper. Transfer to the preheated oven and bake for 15 minutes.

3 Meanwhile, to make the biscuit topping, sift the flour, baking powder, paprika, and salt into a large mixing bowl. Rub in the butter until the mixture resembles fine bread crumbs, then stir in enough of the milk to make a smooth dough. Transfer to a lightly floured work surface, knead lightly, then roll out to a thickness of about ½ inch. Cut out circles using a 2-inch round pastry cutter.

4 Remove the casserole dish from the oven and arrange the dough circles over the top, then return to the oven and bake for 30 minutes, or until the biscuit topping has risen and is lightly golden. Serve immediately.

96

Spinach & Squash Casserole

SERVES 2

2 cups bite-size butternut
   squash cubes

2 small red onions, each cut into
   8 wedges

2 teaspoons vegetable oil

4½ cups baby spinach leaves

1 tablespoon water

2 tablespoons whole-wheat
   bread crumbs

pepper

White sauce

1 cup skim milk

2 tablespoons cornstarch

1 teaspoon dry mustard

1 small onion

2 bay leaves

1 tablespoon grated Parmesan
   or pecorino cheese

Method

1 Preheat the oven to 400°F and put a casserole dish or Dutch oven into the oven to warm up.

2 Arrange the squash and red onions on a baking sheet and coat with the oil and plenty of pepper. Bake in the preheated oven for 20 minutes, turning once.

3 To make the sauce, put the milk into a small saucepan with the cornstarch, dry mustard, onion, and bay leaves. Whisk over medium heat until thick. Remove from the heat, discard the onion and bay leaves, and stir in the cheese. Set aside, stirring occasionally to prevent a skin from forming.

4 When the squash is nearly cooked, put the spinach in a large saucepan with the water and stir over medium heat for 2–3 minutes, or until just wilted.

5 Put half of the squash mixture in the warm casserole dish and top with half of the spinach. Repeat the layers. Pour the white sauce on top and sprinkle with the bread crumbs.

6 Transfer to the preheated oven and bake for 15–20 minutes, until the topping is golden and bubbling. Serve immediately.

97

Vegetable Casserole with Corn

SERVES 4–6

6 tablespoons olive oil or butter

5 onions, finely sliced

3–4 garlic cloves, finely chopped

1 teaspoon cumin seeds

1 teaspoon dried oregano

4 fresh tomatoes, peeled and
   chopped

½ butternut squash peeled, seeded,
   and cut into small dice

4 cups cooked pinto beans or
   cranberry (borlotti) beans,
   drained and rinsed

2 tablespoons pitted and chopped
   green olives

2 tablespoons raisins

1 tablespoon confectioners' sugar

1 teaspoon crushed red pepper

salt and pepper

Topping

8½ cups fresh or frozen corn kernels
   (about 3 pounds)

1½ cups milk

1 egg, beaten

salt and pepper

Method

1 Preheat the oven to 350°F.

2 Heat ¼ cup of the oil in a heavy saucepan, add the onions and garlic, and cook over low heat, stirring occasionally, for 20–30 minutes, or until softened. Add the cumin seeds, oregano, and tomatoes and simmer for 10 minutes, or until a thick sauce has formed.

3 Add the squash and heat until bubbling. Reduce the heat to low, cover, and cook for an additional 10–15 minutes, or until the squash is softened but not collapsed. Stir in the beans, olives, and raisins. Reheat gently and simmer for 5 minutes. Season with salt and pepper.

4 For the topping, put the corn kernels in a blender or food processor with the milk and blend to a paste. Transfer to a saucepan and cook, stirring continuously, for 5 minutes, or until the mixture has thickened slightly. Remove from the heat and let cool. Stir in the egg and season with salt and pepper.

5 Spread the bean mixture in a casserole dish or Dutch oven and top with a thick layer of the corn mixture. Drizzle with the remaining oil and sprinkle with the sugar and crushed red pepper. Bake in the preheated oven for 30 minutes, or until browned and bubbling. Serve immediately.

98

Eggplant Casserole

SERVES 4

4 eggplants

3 tablespoons olive oil, plus extra
  for oiling

10 ounces mozzarella cheese,
  thinly sliced

4 slices prosciutto, shredded

1 teaspoon chopped dried marjoram

¼ cup grated Parmesan cheese

salt and pepper

Tomato sauce

¼ cup olive oil

1 large onion, sliced

4 garlic cloves, crushed

14½-ounce can diced tomatoes

4 ripe tomatoes, peeled and chopped

¼ cup chopped fresh parsley

2½ cups hot vegetable stock

1 tablespoon sugar

2 tablespoons lemon juice

⅔ cup dry white wine

White sauce

2 tablespoons salted butter

3 tablespoons all-purpose flour

1 teaspoon dry mustard

1¼ cups milk

freshly grated nutmeg

Method

1 Preheat the oven to 375°F. Lightly oil a large casserole dish.

2 To make the tomato sauce, heat the oil in a large skillet. Add the onion and garlic and cook until just beginning to soften. Add the canned and fresh tomatoes, parsley, stock, sugar, and lemon juice. Cover and simmer for 15 minutes. Stir in the wine and season with salt and pepper.

3 Thinly slice the eggplants lengthwise. Bring a large saucepan of water to a boil and cook the eggplant slices for 5 minutes. Drain on paper towels.

4 Pour half of the tomato sauce into the prepared dish with half of the eggplants and drizzle with the oil. Cover with half of the mozzarella, prosciutto, and marjoram. Season with salt and pepper. Repeat the layers.

5 To make the white sauce, melt the butter in a large saucepan, then add the flour and dry mustard. Stir until smooth and cook over low heat for 2 minutes. Slowly beat in the milk. Simmer gently for 2 minutes. Remove from the heat, then season with nutmeg and salt and pepper.

6 Spoon the white sauce over the eggplant-and-tomato mixture, then sprinkle with the Parmesan. Bake in the preheated oven for 35–40 minutes, until the topping is golden. Serve immediately.

99

Vegetable Lasagna

SERVES 4

1 eggplant, sliced

3 tablespoons olive oil, plus extra for oiling

2 garlic cloves, crushed

1 red onion, halved and sliced

3 mixed bell peppers, seeded and diced

8 ounces mixed mushrooms, sliced

2 celery stalks, sliced

1 zucchini, diced

½ teaspoon chili powder

½ teaspoon ground cumin

2 tomatoes, chopped

1¼ cups tomato puree

2 tablespoons chopped fresh basil

8 oven-ready lasagna verde noodles

salt and pepper

Cheese sauce

2 tablespoons butter or margarine

1 tablespoon all-purpose flour

⅔ cup vegetable stock

1¼ cups milk

⅔ cup shredded cheddar cheese

1 teaspoon Dijon mustard

1 tablespoon chopped fresh basil

1 egg, beaten

Method

1 Place the eggplant slices in a colander, sprinkle with salt, and let stand for 20 minutes. Rinse under cold water, drain, and reserve.

2 Preheat the oven to 350°F and lightly oil a large casserole dish.

3 Heat the oil in a saucepan. Add the garlic and onion and sauté for 1–2 minutes. Add the bell peppers, mushrooms, celery, and zucchini and cook, stirring thoroughly, for 3–4 minutes. Stir in the chili powder and cumin and cook for 1 minute. Mix in the tomatoes, tomato puree, and basil and season with salt and pepper.

4 For the cheese sauce, melt the butter in a saucepan. Stir in the flour and cook for 1 minute. Remove from the heat and gradually stir in the stock and milk. Return to the heat, then add half of the cheese and all of the mustard. Boil, stirring, until thickened. Stir in the basil. Remove from the heat and stir in the egg.

5 Place half of the lasagna noodles into the prepared dish. Top with half of the vegetable mixture and half of the eggplant slices. Repeat the layers, then spoon the cheese sauce on top. Sprinkle with the remaining cheese and bake in the preheated oven for 40 minutes, or until golden and bubbling. Serve immediately.

100

Vegetable Cannelloni

SERVES 4

12 dried cannelloni tubes

½ cup olive oil, plus extra for oiling

1 eggplant, diced

8 ounces spinach

2 garlic cloves, crushed

1 teaspoon ground cumin

1 cup chopped white button
   mushrooms

2 ounces mozzarella cheese, sliced

salt and pepper

mâche, to garnish

Tomato sauce

1 tablespoon olive oil

1 onion, chopped

2 garlic cloves, crushed

28-ounce can diced tomatoes

1 teaspoon sugar

2 tablespoons chopped fresh basil

Method

1 Preheat the oven to 375°F. Lightly oil a large casserole dish.

2 Bring a large, heavy saucepan of lightly salted water to a boil. Add the cannelloni tubes, return to a boil, and cook for 8–10 minutes, or according to the package directions, until tender but still firm to the bite. Drain on paper towels and pat dry.

3 Heat the oil in a skillet over medium heat. Add the eggplant and cook, stirring frequently, for about 2–3 minutes.

4 Add the spinach, garlic, cumin, and mushrooms and reduce the heat. Season with salt and pepper and cook, stirring, for about 2–3 minutes. Spoon the mixture into the cannelloni tubes and put into the prepared dish in a single layer.

5 To make the tomato sauce, heat the oil in a saucepan over medium heat. Add the onion and garlic and cook for 1 minute. Add the tomatoes, sugar, and basil and bring to a boil. Reduce the heat and simmer for about 5 minutes. Spoon the sauce over the cannelloni tubes.

6 Arrange the mozzarella over the top and bake in the preheated oven for about 30 minutes, or until the cheese is golden brown and bubbling. Serve immediately, garnished with mâche.

Index